WEAPON

THE STEN GUN

LEROY THOMPSON

Series Editor Martin Pegler

First published in Great Britain in 2012 by Osprey Publishing,
PO Box 883, Oxford, OX1 9PL, UK
1385 Broadway, 5th Floor, New York, NY 10018, USA
Email: info@ospreypublishing.com

Osprey Publishing is an imprint of Bloomsbury Publishing Plc

Transferred to digital print on demand 2016

First published 2012
2nd impression 2016

Printed and bound by Cadmus Communications, USA

A CIP catalogue record for this book is available from the British Library

ISBN: 978 1 84908 759 9
PDF eBook ISBN: 978 1 84908 760 5
ePub ISBN: 978 1 78096 125 5

Page layout by Mark Holt
Index by Alan Rutter
Battlescene artwork by Mark Stacey
Cutaway by Alan Gilliland
Typeset in Sabon and Univers
Originated by PDQ Media, Bungay, UK

Osprey Publishing is supporting the Woodland Trust, the UK's leading woodland conservation charity, by funding the dedication of trees.

www.ospreypublishing.com

Acknowledgments

Leroy Thompson would like to thank the following for their assistance in preparing this book: Ken Choate, T.J. Mullin, John Ross, Jon Baker of the Airborne Assault Museum, the US National Archives and Records Administration, the Danish Resistance Museum, the Imperial War Museum, the Library and Archives of Canada and the Rock Island Auction Company.

Mark Stacey would like to thank Captain Peter Laidler of the Small Arms School Corps, Warminster, UK, for generously allowing him to photograph Stens in their collection.

Imperial War Museum Collections

Many of the photos in this book come from the Imperial War Museum's huge collections which cover all aspects of conflict involving Britain and the Commonwealth since the start of the twentieth century. These rich resources are available online to search, browse and buy at www.iwm.org.uk. In addition to Collections Online, you can visit the Visitor Rooms where you can explore over 8 million photographs, thousands of hours of moving images, the largest sound archive of its kind in the world, thousands of diaries and letters written by people in wartime, and a huge reference library. To make an appointment, call (020) 7416 5320, or e-mail mail@iwm.org.uk

Imperial War Museum www.iwm.org.uk

Artist's note

Readers may care to note that the original paintings from which the colour plates in this book were prepared are available for private sale. All reproduction copyright whatsoever is retained by the Publishers. All inquiries should be addressed to:

mark@mrstacey.plus.com

The Publishers regret that they can enter into no correspondence upon this matter.

Editor's note

For ease of comparison please refer to the following conversion table:

1 mile = 1.6km
1yd = 0.9m
1ft = 0.3m
1in. = 2.54cm/25.4mm
1 gallon (US) = 3.8 liters
1 ton (US) = 0.9 metric tons
1lb = 0.45kg

Cover images courtesy of the IWM and the REME Museum of Technology

CONTENTS

INTRODUCTION

In many ways the Sten gun was the perfect weapon for its time and its place. When the Sten was developed during 1941, Great Britain's industrial capacity was strained to the limit and the threat of a German invasion remained a reality. A submachine gun that could be manufactured cheaply and quickly using light machinery in small shops offered an alternative to importing the expensive M1928 Thompson from the United States, especially once the US entered the war and needed Thompsons to arm its own forces. Needing only 48 parts in its simplest version, the Mk III, the Sten primarily used stamped components, with only the bolt and barrel having to be machined. Hence, the Sten required less steel and other materials. Compared to the .45 Thompson, the Sten's chambering in 9mm Parabellum also offered the advantage of requiring less lead, copper and brass in the manufacture of its ammunition. In addition, captured German and Italian 9mm ammunition could be used, although care had to be taken not to mistake Italian 9mm Glisenti for 9mm Parabellum ammunition, as the lighter load of the Glisenti made malfunctions more likely.

The role of the Sten in Britain's armed forces was not unlike that of the US M1 Carbine. Although the semi-auto M1 Garand rifle had been considered for adoption for British forces in 1939, the bolt-action No. 4 Mk I Lee-Enfield was already in production and it was not deemed feasible to switch to a completely new infantry rifle. As a result, this update of the venerable SMLE remained in service through World War II and into the 1950s. Both the Sten and the M1 Carbine found a role among troops who would not normally need the range and power of a rifle, and among those who valued light weight and firepower. The Sten would prove to be a compact arm that would give engineering, signals and other support troops short-range defensive firepower, was issued to officers and NCOs in infantry units, and was widely used by armoured crews. Much as the M1 Carbine would also be adopted by US airborne troops because it was more compact and offered more firepower than a rifle, so the Sten would serve well in the British airborne forces.

For the European Resistance, the Sten proved a most desirable weapon. It was compact and could fit readily into drop containers, be hidden easily or carried concealed, and fired a round that could be obtained from captured German supplies. So easy to fabricate was the Sten that some resistance units built it themselves in garages and bicycle shops. At least some Stens were also supplied to Filipino guerrillas fighting against the Japanese. Not all Stens served with foreign resistance groups, however. Among the first to receive the Sten were members of the top-secret British Auxiliary Units trained to stay behind and act as guerrilla fighters should the Germans invade the UK.

The Sten's effectiveness in Israeli hands during the 1948 War of Independence is one of the best examples of the weapon's simplicity of manufacture, and the ease with which troops could be trained in its use. During the period of the pre-independence British Mandate, Sten guns and 9mm ammunition had been manufactured clandestinely, and the Sten saw wide service during and after 1948. Stens supplied by the British were also used by Arab troops fighting the Israelis. Though superseded by the Uzi from the mid-1950s, the Sten performed an important role in the foundation of Israel.

A Mk II-armed airborne soldier training in the UK during October 1942. (IWM TR 63)

Although only 300,000 Sten Mk I and Mk I*s were produced, more than two million Sten Mk IIs were manufactured. Among the advantages of the Mk II was that it could be suppressed, making it the first widely used suppressed submachine gun. It would remain in service in the 'silent killing' role into the Vietnam War at least and probably longer, with both the US Special Forces and the Australian Special Air Service using the Sten Mk II (S). In British service, the Sten was used at least into the 1960s and saw action in counterinsurgency campaigns in Malaya and Kenya.

The Sten may have been cheap to produce, but it was not always popular with the troops. They found it unreliable and prone to accidental discharge, factors that along with its appearance earned it the nicknames 'Plumber's Abortion', 'Plumber's Nightmare' and 'Stench Gun'. To a large extent, the reliability problems stemmed from the use of the German MP 28/II submachine-gun magazine as a pattern for the Sten's. The system of merging cartridges from two columns to one for feeding was especially sensitive to dirt or deformation of the magazine lips.

Despite the Sten's faults, however, it put small arms into the hands of large numbers of troops who would otherwise have been scrounging for weapons. The Sten's simplicity of design meant that it could be readily and quickly produced in countries without a heavy industrial base, or with a weapons industry already stretched producing rifles, machine guns and other weapons. As a result, it was widely licensed for production in other countries. The Sten was used by at least 35 countries during World War II and afterwards. This even included the Germans, who employed captured Stens and made their own copies.

Estimates of the total number of Stens built run as high as 4.5 million or even more of all variants. As with other weapons supplied to resistance groups a substantial portion were 'lost', although it is amazing to note how many of those lost Stens or other weapons still turn up in France, Italy, the Philippines and elsewhere. Many were hidden away just in case of future need, as those who had been conquered by the Germans or Japanese often decided they would not be unarmed 'the next time'. Because there were so many Stens made, since World War II they have often turned up in the wrong hands. The IRA, for example, has used Stens and so have insurgents in Cyprus, Kenya, Malaya and elsewhere.

The combat use of the Sten offers striking contrasts as they were issued to two groups with widely differing missions. In many cases, submachine guns were issued to military police, armoured crews, weapons crews, support troops, or others likely to use their weapons only if overrun or in other emergency situations. On the other hand, the Sten has been used by airborne troops, guerrilla fighters and special-operations personnel who were likely to use their weapons up close against the enemy. As a result, experiences of users vary – from the Sten serving as a faithful companion never fired in anger, to recollections of the weapon as an efficient silent killer used to eliminate numerous enemy troops.

Certainly it ranks as an important development in the history of the submachine gun.

DEVELOPMENT

A sheet-metal submachine gun

At least some World War I tacticians believed that the development of a portable machine gun which troops could fire as they advanced would help break the stalemate on the Western Front. Use of the Bergmann MP 18 by German 'storm troopers' during breakthroughs in 1918 seemed to validate the concept. The US Pederson Device, which converted the M1903 Springfield rifle to a semi-automatic weapon that could be fired during the advance, was a related development. The Thompson was another submachine gun that can trace its genesis to the desire to give the World War I infantryman more firepower. Developed by Gen John Thompson, it would not however enter production until 1921. During the period between the wars, other designs of compact, pistol-calibre automatic 'carbines' proliferated.

The British Army had shown some interest in the submachine gun during World War I. The twin-barrelled Italian 9mm Villar-Perosa – originally designed for use in aeroplanes, but generally accepted as the first submachine gun – was demonstrated at the School of Musketry (from 1919 called the Small Arms School, then from 1929 called the Small Arms School Corps) in Hythe, Kent, in October 1915. After a trial at Royal Small Arms Factory (RSAF) Enfield in October 1915, the Villar-Perosa was given a favourable report; however, General Headquarters in France saw no advantage to an increase in the number of weapon types in use.

Other submachine guns were tested during the years between the wars, including the .45 ACP US M1921 Thompson in June 1921. Although the Thompson performed well, it was not adopted at that time. In 1926, Birmingham Small Arms (BSA) developed a version of the Thompson chambered for the 9×20mm cartridge (aka 9mm Browning Long). It is interesting that this cartridge was chosen in preference to the standard .45

Weapons terminology

The terms 'submachine gun', 'machine carbine' and 'machine pistol' are often used interchangeably and can be quite confusing. 'Submachine gun' is the most widely used term and applies to weapons from the Thompson to the Sten gun to the HK MP5 in use today. Generally, the term is applied to select-fire or full-automatic weapons with relatively short barrels firing a pistol-calibre cartridge. 'Machine carbine' seems to have been the term widely used in World War II British Ordnance circles to describe the submachine gun. However, 'machine carbine' has also been used to describe weapons such as the Russian AKSU or German HK53, which are submachine guns chambered for rifle cartridges. The Germans used the term 'machine pistol' to describe a submachine gun, but it is more generally used to describe pistols that have a select-fire capability and are often equipped with a shoulder stock. The Russian Stechkin or the select-fire Mauser M1896 pistols are good examples. In this book the term 'submachine gun' is used to describe the Sten and comparable weapons.

ACP used in the Thompson or the 9mm Parabellum round. No reason for the choice is given in the sources consulted, but it may be surmised that the 9×20mm may have been chosen because of lower recoil. The BSA version was tested in 1928 with the Cutts compensator, a recoil brake that forced the barrel downward against muzzle rise, but did not generate much interest.

An improved version of the Villar-Perosa, now with a single barrel, was tested in April 1928, but nothing seems to have come of this. Other submachine guns were tested by the British during the 1930s, including the German 9mm Vollmer (in 1932), Swiss 9mm Solothurn S1-100 (December 1934), Finnish 9mm Konepistooli kp/31 'Suomi' (September 1936), American .45 ACP Hyde Model 1935 (June 1937), Spanish 7.65mm Star (1937), and Japanese 8mm Type 1 Nambu (1938). Evaluations of the Suomi were relatively positive, which is logical as it is generally rated one of the best submachine guns ever produced – well made, hard-wearing and dependable, even in the extreme cold of the Finnish winter. The Small Arms Committee (SAC) report on the Suomi rated it one of the best 'gangster weapons' that they had evaluated. The terminology demonstrates the SAC's preconceived view of the submachine gun!

In March 1938, a gas-operated 7.63mm submachine gun from Brøndby in Denmark was tested and was deemed to 'show promise' by the SAC. As a result, trials were planned to test submachine guns firing the .45 ACP, 9mm Parabellum, 7.63mm Mauser and 9mm Mauser rounds to evaluate ammunition for submachine guns. These trials would have included the Hyde, Suomi, Solothurn, Schmeisser MP 28/II, Bergmann and Brøndby. Seemingly, however, the trials never took place.

Also tested in 1938 was the 9mm Biwarip submachine gun, although actually it was more of a machine pistol (see box above). Deemed too light to be used effectively, and apparently having no provision for a shoulder stock, the Biwarip did however incorporate two features which would be used on the Sten – a ventilated barrel shroud and a side-feeding magazine.

The Suomi had left enough of a positive impression that in October 1938 a later version was tested. Its performance was viewed positively and evaluators were particularly impressed with the 50-round 'coffin' magazine (so designated because of its shape) – so much so that they

The 9mm kp/31 'Suomi' was viewed very favourably by British Ordnance personnel during the evaluations of different 'machine carbines'. Although a Finnish design, there were variants such as this shorter-barrelled Swedish one. 35,000 were made under licence by Sweden's Husqvarna Vapenfabriks AB just before and during World War II; some were also imported from Finland. Designated kpist m/37 (9mm Browning Long calibre) after the year of adaption, in 1939 Sweden decided to switch to 9mm Parabellum and the new weapons were designated kpist m/37-39. (Author)

looked into the possibility of making a Bren magazine of the same type. However, it was still decided that a 'machine carbine' was not needed. The British General Staff continued to prefer the general issue of rifles, which had greater lethality, penetration and range.

This attitude continued until the outbreak of World War II, although in May 1939, the Ordnance Board (replacing the SAC in evaluating designs) showed interest in the Hungarian 9mm Kiraly design, which would later become the Hungarian M39 submachine gun. It was deemed too complicated, but suggestions were made with regard to improving its unwieldy 40-round fixed magazine and its complicated and intricate firing mechanism, and consideration was given to its production by BSA. In May 1939 the Director of Artillery wrote to the Secretary of the Ordnance Board requesting that an order for 1,000 German Erma EMP submachine guns be investigated, because they could be acquired quickly, but four months later Britain was at war with Germany, and no order was placed.

THE OUTBREAK OF WAR

Once again plunged into conflict with Germany, in December 1939 the British Expeditionary Force in France urgently requested submachine guns. Although the Ordnance Board considered the Suomi the best choice, it was assumed that it would be difficult to obtain the weapon since Finland was fighting for its existence in the Winter War (November 1939–March 1940) against the Soviet Union and needed every weapon available. Although Sweden also produced the Suomi on licence, production was probably too limited to meet British demand.

As a result, early in 1940 the decision was made to adopt the US Thompson submachine gun, presumably the M1928, to meet current needs; the .45 ACP cartridge was already a British service cartridge, as Colt 1911A1 pistols were widely issued during World War II. Since the United States was not yet at war, it was believed shipments could be received quickly. From April 1940, 107,000 Thompsons were ordered, each with two 50-round drums and four 20-round box magazines, eventually reaching a total of around 300,000. (According to Laidler

(Laidler 2000: 3) only one-third of those ordered actually reached the UK, with 100,000 reportedly going down on a single ship.) The increasing pace of US rearmament as war became more likely, which gave priority to domestic needs, meant that by the end of 1940 the receipt of British Thompsons totalled only 107,500.

Britain's first submachine gun: the Lanchester

After the evacuation of Dunkirk in May–June 1940 and with an invasion of the British Isles expected, the need for weapons to counter the expected German airborne assaults or amphibious landings became desperate. Although the Army had decided upon the Thompson submachine gun, both the RAF and the Royal Navy wanted submachine guns to defend air and naval facilities. In August 1940, it was decided that 50,000 British copies of the German 9mm MP 28/II would be produced to meet immediate demands. The two MP 28/IIs that were copied had been acquired by the British Consul in Addis Ababa, Ethiopia (Laidler 1995: 3). Sterling Armament Company in Dagenham, East London, was chosen to produce them as quickly as possible, and by early November had two prototypes ready for testing. Some minor changes were requested and a few days later they were tested again. Though there were some failures to fire, the prototypes were deemed worthy of more rigorous trials.

Endurance trials began on 28 November 1940 with the test gun passing proof[1] and functioning trials. Although there were 26 stoppages in 5,204 rounds, these were mostly attributed to the use of 9mm Beretta ammunition, which had a longer case. It fired reliably with seven other types including German military issue. The British 'Schmeisser' also passed mud and sand tests as well as accuracy tests. Ready for production as the Lanchester Mk I, it was named after the engineer who developed and supervised production of the British version, George H. Lanchester. Initially it went into production at Sterling Engineering under the supervision

BELOW
A Lanchester Mk I*. The Lanchester, based on the German MP 28/II, was the first British submachine gun developed during World War II. It was used primarily by the Royal Navy. (John Ross)

BOTTOM
A top view of a Lanchester Mk I* with magazine fitted. Note the brass magazine housing, which is handsome but also expensive. (John Ross)

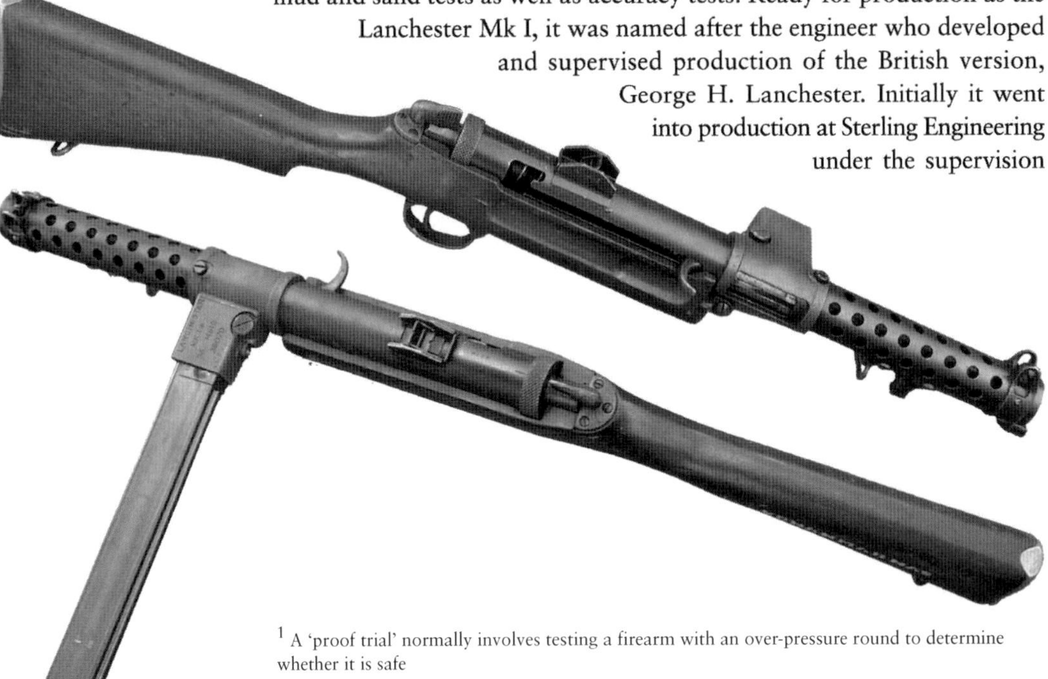

[1] A 'proof trial' normally involves testing a firearm with an over-pressure round to determine whether it is safe

of George Lanchester, though there were more than 70 subcontractors. Some Lanchesters were also assembled at established gunmakers W.W. Greener of Chippenham, and Boss & Co. of London, with all production slated to go to the Royal Navy. (There is evidence, however, that at least some Lanchesters were used by members of the Royal Artillery in India and later by the Kenya Police during the Mau Mau Uprising (Laidler 1995: 7).

As produced, the Mk I was a copy of the MP 28/II with minor alterations. It took a 50-round magazine that protruded from the left side, but could also use Sten 32-round magazines. The simplified Mk I*, which replaced the Mk I in early 1942, did away with the selector and was only capable of being fired on full-automatic. Many Mk I Lanchesters were converted to Mk I* configuration. The initial order of 50,000 was intended to be split evenly between the Royal Navy and the Royal Air Force. However, the RAF had acquired 2,000 Smith & Wesson 9mm carbines from the United States, which helped fill the gap. As a result, all or most of the 80,000 Lanchesters eventually produced went to the Royal Navy. Laidler actually speculates that the number of 80,000 is low, in that the total produced by Sterling was at least 74,579, while Greener produced 16,990 and Boss 3,900. It is possible that the 80,000 figure often cited was based just on Sterling production (Laidler 1995: 18–19). It is interesting to note that the Lanchester was not declared obsolete by the Royal Navy until 1978–79. Some Royal Navy ships sold during the 1950s and 1960s contained Lanchesters as part of the stores that went with the ships. As a result, some foreign nations requested spare parts from Sterling at least into the 1970s (Laidler 1995: 24–25).

As might be expected of a submachine gun based on a 1920s-era German design, the Lanchester required a substantial amount of machining. It used expensive materials as well; the magazine housing, for example, was made of solid brass. Another important consideration is that production of the Lanchester averaged only about 3,400 per month. In comparison, during one week in 1943, the BSA plant at Tyseley assembled 47,000 Mk II Stens (Laidler 1995: 7). Lanchester production would cease entirely in October 1943, for even as the Lanchester was being developed, a much simpler submachine gun had been designed. This was ready to be demonstrated in January 1941.

THE STEN ENTERS THE SCENE

In the months after Dunkirk the need for a lightweight, easily portable infantry weapon that could be quickly and cheaply produced and deliver a lot of close-range firepower was apparent, but the Ministry of Supply emphasised that there were no milling machines available for use on a new design. (Milling machines move the piece which is being formed against the rotating milling cutter, which cuts on the sides as well as the tip.) The genesis of the Sten was reportedly a sketch for a simplified trigger mechanism, made in early December 1940 by H.J. Turpin, senior draughtsman at RSAF Enfield. With only two moving parts, this trigger

A pilot model of the Sten (serial number 17). Note the vertical foregrip, the wooden forearm and insert in the skeleton grip, and the cone-shaped flash suppressor. As with other early Stens the safety requires that the bolt be rotated downwards, rather than upwards as on the Mk II. (Copyright Collector Grade Publications, Inc.)

mechanism would be perfect for an inexpensive submachine-gun design. This evolved into a design for a 'street fighting machine carbine' that could be produced with minimal machine tools using stampings and unskilled labour. The new design's compactness, lightness and ease of production were all considered advantages.

An early tool-room example was quickly built at RSAF Enfield employing a tube normally used for a Vickers medium machine gun's tripod leg as a receiver. It successfully fired 100 rounds during a demonstration, and so by 1 February 1941 the Imperial General Staff asked the Ministry of Supply for 100,000 of the weapon. Two further prototypes were built at the Philco Radio Works at Perivale, Middlesex, and were ready during early 1941. Major Hearn-Cooper, an experienced mechanical and production engineer, was charged with building the two prototypes, designated T40 (1) and T40 (2). A T40 prototype did well during a demonstration at Aldershot, Hampshire – carried out by two Scots Guardsmen, one armed with a rifle and one with a Sten prototype, who demonstrated speed of fire on a moving dummy – and in a 5,000-round endurance and functioning test of January 1941 at the Small Arms School at Hythe, Kent, with the results being viewed as favourable enough to merit production. In fact, in a 24 January 1941 official minute from the Imperial General Staff, the new 'machine carbine' was described as 'one of the best bits of design on small arms carried out in England for a very long time' (Laidler 2000: 16). The fact that five of these submachine guns could be produced for the price of one Lanchester and 15 for the price of one Thompson made it even more attractive to the financially strapped British government, which had been using its precious gold reserves to purchase Thompsons.

Once manufacture of the weapon was approved, Hearn-Cooper was responsible for getting it into mass production. Aided by experts in machining, machine tools and metal pressing, Hearn-Cooper sought manufacturers for the 59 component parts of the new weapon. It was named the STEN: the 'S' was taken from the surname of Maj Reginald V. Shepherd, who was Inspector of Armaments in the Ministry of Supply Design Department at the Royal Arsenal, Woolwich; the 'T' was from Harold J. Turpin, the designer; and the 'EN' was from the first two letters of Enfield (RSAF Enfield, Middlesex).

Two members of the Dorking Home Guard, one armed with an M1928 Thompson and the other with a Mk I Bren light machine gun, 1 December 1940. (IWM H 5839)

Next, 46 'pilot' models were made at RSAF Enfield. This allowed the sub-assemblies to be built and the drawings adjusted to reflect tolerances and a set of working plans to be made. Using these drawings, the pilot models would be produced to develop tooling and manufacturing techniques for the carbine, at that point still known as the 'ST Machine Carbine'. At this point, it was felt that the Sten would not be suitable for the infantry, which would continue to use the Thompson. On 7 March 1941 the 'Carbine, Machine, Sten, Mk I' was approved for issuance.

THE STEN Mk I AND Mk I*

A 9×19mm weapon, the Sten Mk I was blowback operated with a fixed firing pin. (Once adopted as a standard round, 9mm ammunition was designated 'Cartridge, Small-arms, Ball, 9mm Mk1Z'.) As with the Lanchester, a side-mounted magazine was employed. Initially, the magazine was copied from the German MP 28/II, based on the theory that captured German magazines (and Lanchester magazines) could be used. Early (Mk I) Sten magazines had viewing holes to check the number of cartridges remaining, but these holes allowed debris to get into the magazine, causing the follower to bind. These holes were eliminated on the Mk II Sten magazine. Also, Mk I magazines had a follower that was not braced on the 'U' with a strut. This also caused it to bind. As a result, the Mk II magazine incorporated a bracing strut. The double-column, single-feed design, however, led to unreliability, as the system of having two rows of cartridges merge to one row for feed also made the magazine very susceptible to dirt or slight denting of the magazine, which caused malfunctions. Although the Mk II magazines improved reliability, the basic design for merging two rows of cartridges into one remained flawed.

A magazine-loading device was also deemed necessary (see box on page 27) due to increasing magazine-spring pressure as the magazine became close to full. Only a rudimentary safety, which engaged the bolt in a slot when it was to the rear, was used. However, when the bolt was in the closed position on an empty chamber, if the butt sharply impacted against a hard surface (such as the ground, or the interior of an armoured vehicle), the bolt could be jarred back enough to chamber a round, resulting in an accidental discharge. The Mk I incorporated a crossbolt fire selector that allowed semi-automatic fire (pushed to the right) or full-automatic fire (pushed to the left). Among the distinctive features of the Mk I were a conical 'spoon bill' flash hider with a downward slant, a wooden handguard and a folding vertical foregrip.

Contracts for production of the Sten Mk I were given to the Singer Manufacturing Company in Scotland. This was the Singer Sewing Machine Company, which before World War II was a subsidiary of the US Singer Sewing Machine Company. The company was nationalized by the British government prior to 6 March 1941, when the first contract for 100,000 Sten Mk Is was awarded, followed by a contract for another 100,000 on 1 April 1942. On 22 October 1942 yet another contract was awarded for 100,000 modified versions of the Sten, designated Mk I*. At some point, Singer was awarded a contract for an additional 149 guns, probably to use up spare parts.

In about 1943, workers assemble Mk IIs at ROF Fazakerley, near Liverpool. It was essential that each part fitted perfectly and was not too loose or tight. If parts did not fit easily, they would be rejected as, according to the original caption, 'A man's life, or the life of a platoon or a company may depend on good workmanship.' (IWM D 12370)

Sten ammunition

In 1941 there was a limited production capability for 9mm ammunition at Britain's Imperial Chemical Industries (ICI), but to meet the initial shortage of 9mm ammunition, 110 million rounds were ordered from the USA, from Western Cartridge Company, IL. By late in 1941, production capacity in the UK had been expanded and the 'Cartridge Small Arms, Ball, 9mm Mk1Z' had been introduced. Since the Royal Navy was already using the Lanchester, this cartridge had been designed to Naval design specifications. The Mk1Z round was initially produced at the Royal Laboratory, Woolwich Arsenal, and later produced at ROF Blackpole in Worcestershire.

In September 1943, the Mk 2Z cartridge was introduced, which resulted in the Mk 1Z being declared obsolescent in November 1944 (Laidler 2000: 12). The Mk 2Z load was based very closely upon German ammunition captured in North Africa and was known for being a heavy load better suited to the submachine gun than the pistol. The Mk 2Z used a 115-grain bullet travelling at 1,300 feet per second, which created 431ft/lb of muzzle energy; in contrast, the .45 ACP uses a 230-grain bullet at 820 feet per second, which creates 350ft/lb of muzzle energy. Note that muzzle-energy figures are often misleading and that the .45 ACP full-metal-jacketed service round has normally proven a better manstopper than the 9mm full-metal-jacket service round. The Mk2Z continued as the British service 9mm round after World War II even though it was hard (owing to heavy recoil) on the L9A1 pistol, otherwise known as the Browning Hi-Power, the standard-issue British service pistol (Laidler 2000: 35).

The Mk I* Sten eliminated the flash hider and the wooden handguard as well as the vertical foregrip. Instead of the wooden handguard, a stamped cover for the trigger group also acted as the handguard. In addition to those Stens manufactured as Mk I*s, some Mk Is were also armourer-modified to this configuration as the wooden handguards and vertical foregrips were no longer available. In some cases, the stamped handguard was used, but the flash hider remained. Some of the 300,149 Mk I and Mk I* Stens produced were subsequently modified to take the Mk V cocking handle. The Mk I and Mk I* versions were finally declared obsolete in September 1947.

THE STEN Mk II

The Mk I and Mk I* were succeeded by the Mk II primarily because the earlier designs were considered 'complicated', each weapon requiring 12 man-hours to produce. As a result, the Design and Development Department at RSAF Enfield worked to simplify the design so it would lend itself more readily to mass production. Nevertheless, the Mk II's basic design and configuration remained almost the same as the Mk I*. Also contributing to the Mk II design was a 24 March 1941 request to make the Sten capable of ready disassembly for use by airborne troops. The incorporation of two collars for quick removal of the barrel and the butt stock allowed users to easily disassemble the Mk II for stowage in a parachute harness or 'leg bag'. Also useful for airborne troops was the design of the Mk II's magazine well, which unlike that of the Mk I could be rotated downwards, decreasing the weapon's width by about half. Another advantage of this rotating magazine well was that when it was rotated 90 degrees to the vertical position, the housing acted as a dust cover for the ejection port. (Note, however, that the 32-round Sten magazine could not seat when the magazine well was rotated to the

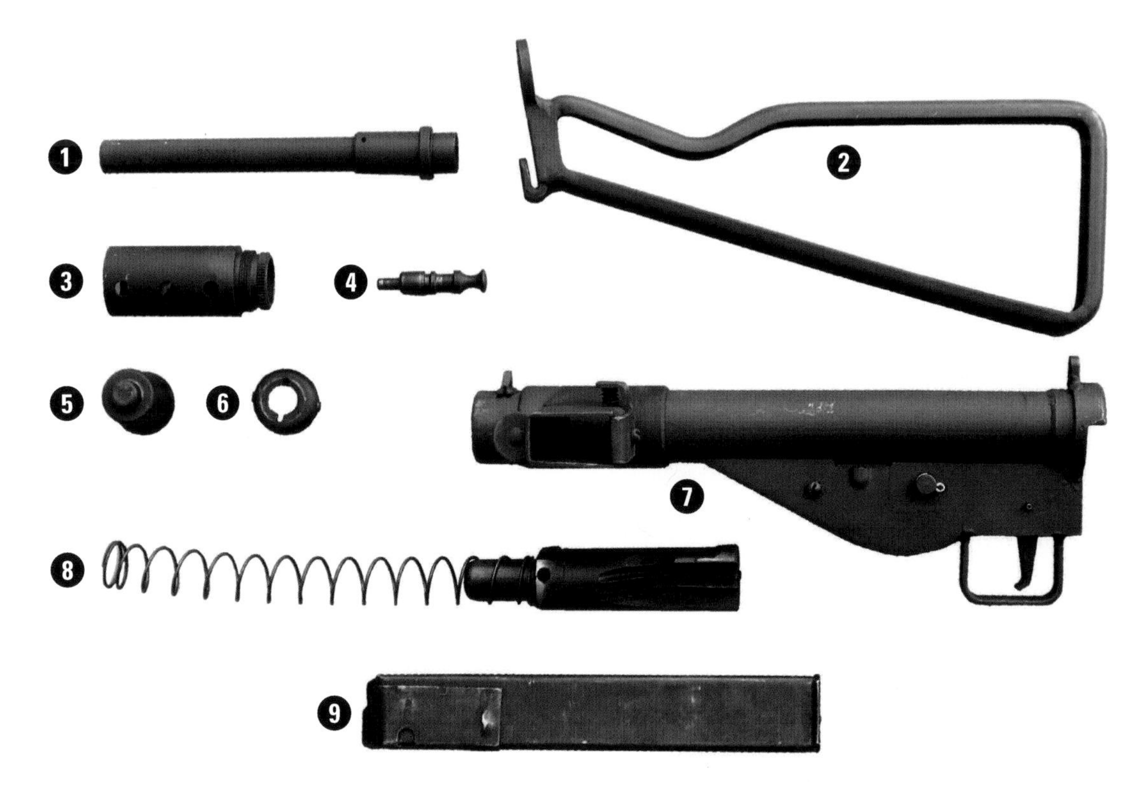

A Mk II disassembled into its primary component parts: **(1)** barrel; **(2)** stock; **(3)** barrel shroud; **(4)** cocking handle; **(5)** locking stud; **(6)** return-spring cap; **(7)** receiver; **(8)** breech block and return spring; **(9)** magazine.

vertical position.) Still another feature of the Mk II that allowed it to be stowed more readily was the use of a shorter, 2.125in cocking handle, designated the Mk II (the Mk I was 2.5in long).

Prototype Mk IIs were tested at the end of June and beginning of July 1941. As is often the case with prototype guns, some reliability problems were encountered, many traceable to the ammunition; apparently it was underpowered, which could be readily fixed by changing the powder and/or charge. It was also found that the barrel face was being hammered by the breech block, which required a 'fix' before production began. Production of the Mk II was to be an international effort and so copies of the Mk II drawings were sent to factories in Australia, New Zealand, Canada and India. Contracts for Mk II Stens were awarded to four manufacturers, which were contracted for the following numbers: Royal Ordnance Factory (ROF) Fazakerley – 1,083,000; BSA Guns Ltd, Birmingham – 404,383; ROF Theale – 95,000; Small Arms Ltd (based at Long Branch, Toronto) – 17,000. Other Mk II Stens were manufactured at RSAF Enfield and Wellington, New Zealand. In all, a total of 2,600,000 Mk II Stens were produced.

A view of a Mk II's rear sight; note the chequering to deaden glare. Note, too, the return-spring cap. When it is depressed the stock may be removed; for further disassembly it is pressed and rotated to the right to remove it and the return spring. (Author)

In addition to those changes mentioned above that helped make the Mk II 'paratrooper friendly', there were some other noteworthy changes. The safety slot into which the cocking handle was placed to render the Sten safe, for example, was changed from being down on the Mk I and Mk I* to up on the Mk II. This resulted from a change in the way troops were instructed in the use of the Sten. Originally, they had been taught to cock the weapon with the right hand, then push the cocking handle downward into the safety slot. However, experience showed that it was more effective to cock the Sten with the left hand while holding the stock with the right hand and canting the weapon to the side. It was easier to push the cocking handle upward into the safety slot from this position. The author has also found that it is quicker to slap the cocking handle down out of the slot to prepare it for action.

One problem that became apparent with the detachable barrel system on the Mk II was that after stripping, barrels could be replaced in any position around a 360-degree circle; this could affect the zero of the carbine. As a result, once a barrel was initially zeroed it was marked along the top to show the proper re-assembly position. Barrels with two rifling grooves instead of the six previously used on the Mk I and Mk I* also came into use on the Mk II. Barrel manufacture required machinery designed for rifling; hence, barrel supply, if subcontracted, was sometimes, though not always, carried out by firms in the gun trade. Mk I and Mk III barrels, for example, were produced by Webley & Scott of Birmingham. The production of cold hammer-forged barrels using hardened steel mandrels by Accles & Pollock of Oldbury, Worcestershire, and Power

Changes in stock design

Various changes were made during Sten production with the most visible probably being the four different stock designs: the original Mk I No. 2 tubular stock (BE 9958); the Mk II 'T'-stock (BE 9952); the Mk II No. 3 'loop' or 'skeleton' stock (BE 8324); and finally the Mk III wooden stock (BE 8347) on the Sten Mk V. Note that the Mk 1 No. 1 butt with flat steel skeleton stock with a wooden insert was used on prototype Mk I Stens, but it was never really a production item and is not listed in the first Sten Parts List (Laidler 2000: 18).

The Mk II No. 3 'skeleton' stock allowed stowage of a Sten spike bayonet or a cleaning rod. Although different Sten marques will be encountered with more than one version of the stock, the stocks are not completely interchangeable. For example, the Mk II No. 3 'skeleton' stock will usually fit any of the marques, but the Mk II 'T'-stock will not. Having said that, if it was necessary to use the parts on hand, armourers could make any stock type fit any Sten with some filing and hand-work. In other cases, stocks that would interchange might be used on other Sten marques. For example, the author has seen quite a few Mk II Stens fitted with the Mk III stock and pistol grip (BE 8356) from the Mk V.

Versions of the Sten produced without stocks and fitted with pistol grips were built by European Resistance members to allow better concealment. However, there were also British examples of the Sten designed to use only the pistol grip. Versions of the Sten Mk V with a special cover plate to retain the bolt were available with just a pistol grip for concealment use. Some of these were fitted with suppressors. To allow more control when firing, the later version of the cover plate was fitted with a loop for a Sten sling.

ABOVE This Mk II is fitted with the 'T'-stock more commonly encountered on the Mk III Sten. (Royal Electrical and Mechanical Engineers (REME) Museum)

A Mk II broken into three components for parachuting: stock, receiver and barrel, and magazine. By rotating the magazine well, it did not protrude and the action was protected against debris entering through the magazine-well; however, before the Sten could be brought into action it had to be rotated back into firing position and locked in place. (Author)

Samos Accounting Machines, however, precluded the need for specialized rifling machines.

Various other minor changes were made during the production of the Mk II, including to the ejector, breech block and 'skeleton' butt. Quite a useful improvement was the availability of three heights of front sight (0.53in, 0.56in and 0.59in blade heights when measured from base), which could be chosen either by the manufacturer or later by armourers; the different heights of sight allowed the weapon to be zeroed for elevation more readily.

With the Mk II, production was designed to use semi-skilled workers using jigs to aid fitting. Parts were made at numerous small

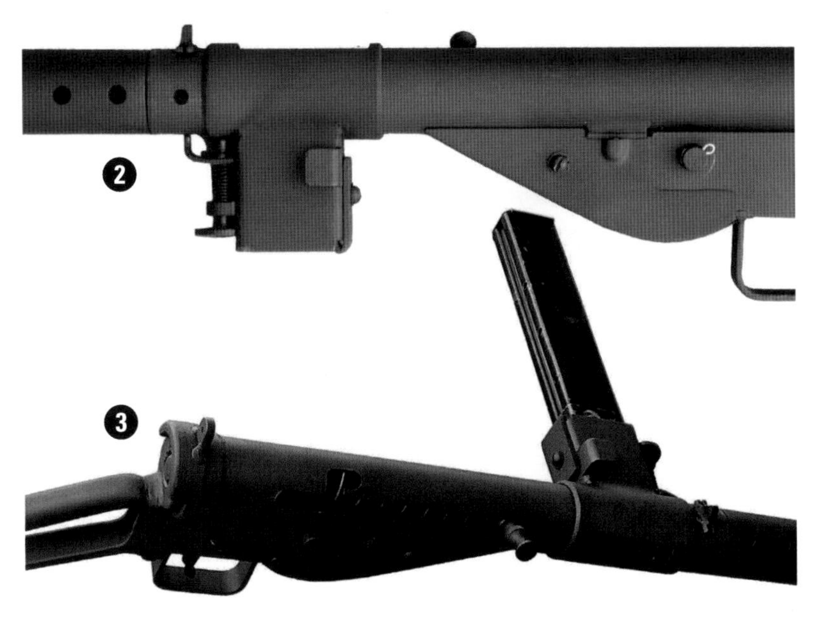

1. This close-up of a Mk II shows the magazine-release lever (right) and the spring-operated release to rotate the magazine well (left). (Author)

2. This Mk II has the magazine well rotated for ease of storage in a drop container. Drop containers were used to drop Stens, ammunition, grenades, explosives, handguns, radio parts and other items to Resistance fighters in France, Denmark and other occupied countries. (Author)

3. This right-side view shows the Safety slot on a Mk II; the cocking handle was pulled back and rotated up into the slot. However, it could jar free, allowing the weapon to discharge. (Author)

THE STEN EXPOSED

Cutaway key

1 Butt stock, Mk II
2 Return-spring housing
3 Rear sight
4 Return spring
5 Safety slot
6 Cocking handle
7 Extractor pin
8 Extractor
9 Firing pin
10 Bullet
11 Cartridge
12 Breech block (forward, ignition position)
13 Ejection port
14 Trigger-housing cover
15 Sear, Mk I
16 Tripping lever
17 Trigger spring
18 Change lever
19 Trigger pin
20 Trigger
21 Sling
22 Barrel
23 Barrel nut
24 Front sight
25 Magazine latch and spring
26 Breech block (rear, cocked position)
27 Return-spring housing
28 Trigger
29 Trigger pin
30 Tripping-lever pin
31 Trigger spring
32 Tripping lever
33 Tripping-lever pawl
34 Sear, Mk I
35 Magazine-housing spacer
36 Magazine housing
37 Barrel-sleeve latch plunger
38 Barrel-sleeve latch
39 Bayonet scabbard
40 Bayonet, Mk I
41 Magazine (top view)
42 Magazine follower
43 Magazine spring

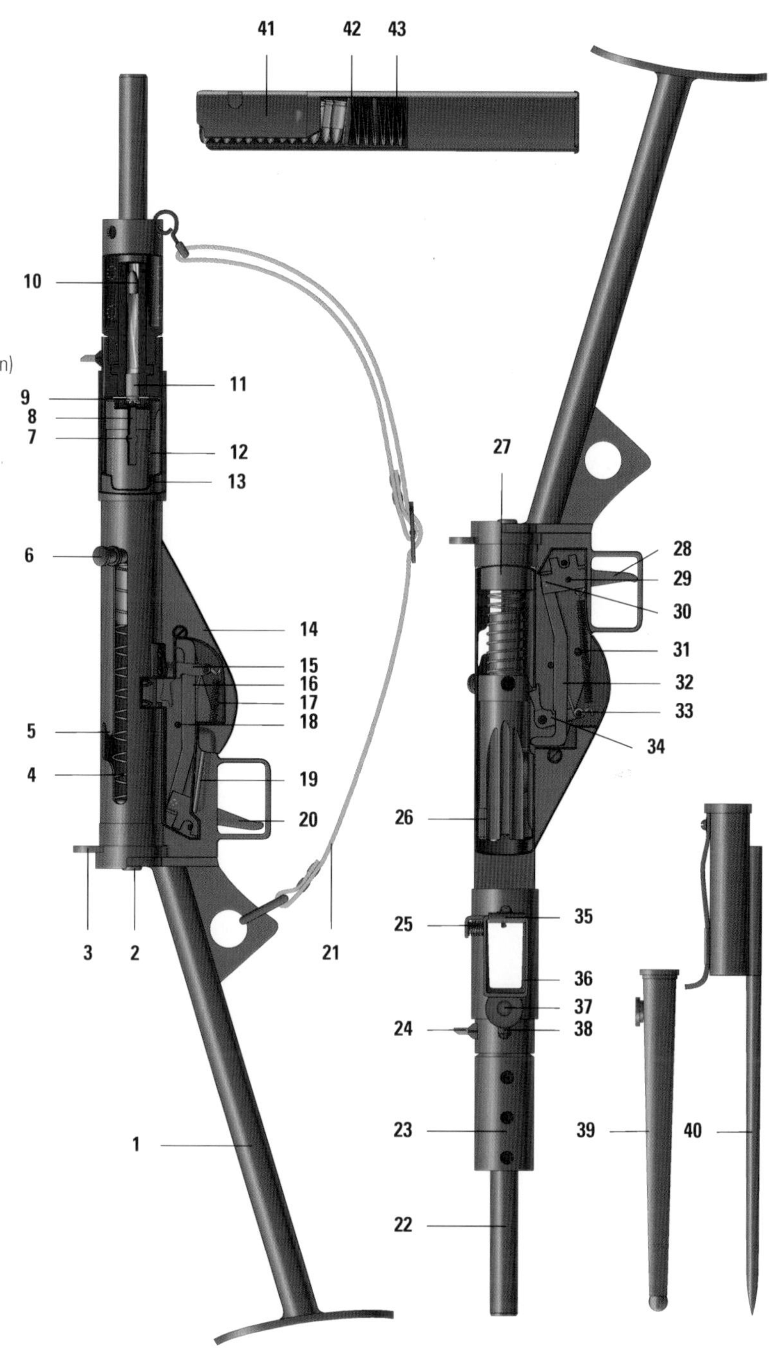

factories – reportedly 100 or more – and sent to the major assemblers, which produced the finished carbines. A truck made the rounds of the small shops each day dropping off raw materials and collecting parts. An 18 September 1943 article in the popular US weekly magazine *Collier's* describes the subcontracting of small parts in village workshops:

> ... Given a free hand, the young man [made responsible for Sten production] broke all the rules in the mass-production rule book. He found garages that could make the sheet-metal tubing, cellar workshops that could machine breech blocks, a pram factory that could make the stock. In one town, he found an empty henhouse where he set up a capstan lathe and some drills to make rough cuts on barrels, and he got enough volunteers from the town's married women to keep them busy night and day.
>
> Stables, laundries, lofts, even the garrets of homes became tiny workshops. Machines that couldn't make fine cuts were used for making rough ones. The better-equipped shops handled all the final tooling. Within the spate of a few weeks, he had over 300 workshops, such as they were, making Sten gun parts, and the guns were being assembled at government ordnance factories in mass quantities by early December. The guns seemed to be coming out of nowhere, and no one was more surprised than munitions officials. (Henderson & Shaw 1943: 64)

In some cases, these small workshops made slight adjustments to parts that made them more effective and were adopted as an improvement to production techniques. Since any savings in production time or materials

German and Hungarian women work on the manufacture of Stens, probably Mk IIs, at an ordnance factory, 'somewhere in Britain'. (IWM P 869)

Canadian Stens

Canada's newly established Small Arms Ltd, based at Long Branch, Toronto, received the first Mk II contract, in August 1941, for 17,000 guns. To help get manufacturing under way, BSA personnel helped set up Sten production, including the use of 'cells' of employees working together to assemble the finished Sten. Small Arms Ltd delivered a total of 104,553 Mk IIs by June 1944; after D-Day, Sten production at Long Branch slowed, with only another 25,187 being delivered by September 1945. Further orders were cancelled at this point; however, another 6,797 Stens were produced from parts on hand. Of the Canadian Stens produced, well over half – 72,002 – were sent as aid to China; some of these came back to haunt Canadian and British troops in Korea as they faced North Koreans armed with Long Branch-produced Stens. 1,100,000 Sten magazines were also produced at Long Branch. Because of the plentiful supply of timber in Canada, Small Arms Ltd was contracted in November 1944 to supply 300,000 sets of wood stock blanks for the Mk V Sten. By the time this contract was cancelled in August 1945, slightly over 300,000 sets had been delivered to the UK.

An interesting Canadian Sten variation is the 'Carbine m/c Sten, 9mm CDN Mk2/1'. These comprised 600 Mk II Stens that had their 'skeleton' stocks converted to pistol grips to create a fast-handling weapon for airborne troops that could be quickly brought into action upon landing. However, as this type of Sten did not allow shoulder firing, it was determined that airborne troops would need access to other weapons for sustained combat.

ABOVE This corporal of The Perth Regiment of Canada, a motorized infantry regiment that served with Canadian 5th Armoured Division in Italy and (from March 1945) the Low Countries, is armed with the Canadian-produced Mk II. (Library and Archives of Canada)

was considered relevant in maximizing Sten production, even the smallest improvement was desirable. On the other hand, attempts to increase production led to quality-control problems with the Sten by late 1942. Subsequently, an increased emphasis on quality control led to a shortfall of over 400,000–600,000 Stens during 1943 (the production target for 1943 was 1.5 million). Nevertheless, quality control did improve.

THE STEN Mk III

Although the Sten Mk II continued in production through 1943, another 'improved' marque, the Mk III, had by now been developed by Lines Brothers, Ltd, which had manufactured a large number of parts for the Mk I and Mk I*. Lines Brothers engineers were experts in stampings and had analyzed the Mk I; they determined that they could produce a Sten entirely themselves using stampings that had all holes pre-punched while the stampings were flat, thus eliminating the need for drilling. Prototypes were available by early 1942. As is often the case with prototype weapons, there were a substantial number of malfunctions, but Lines Brothers tweaked the design. After some changes to the ejection port including

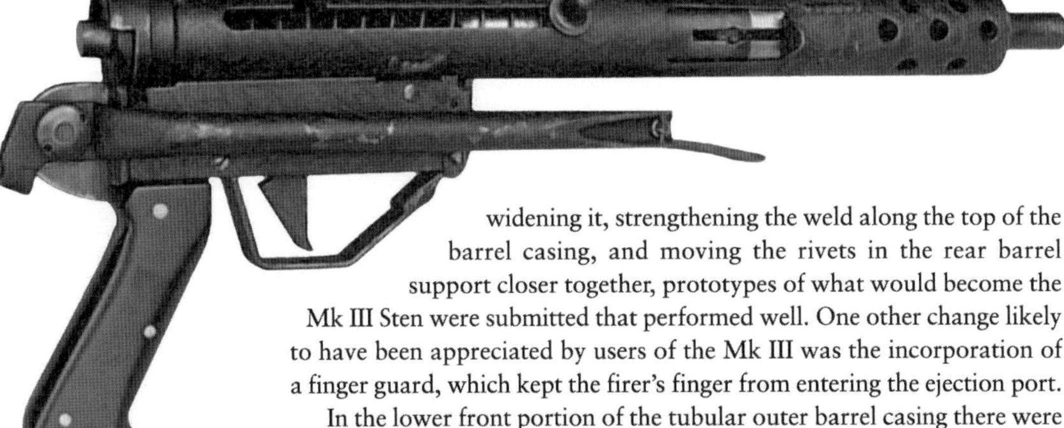

widening it, strengthening the weld along the top of the barrel casing, and moving the rivets in the rear barrel support closer together, prototypes of what would become the Mk III Sten were submitted that performed well. One other change likely to have been appreciated by users of the Mk III was the incorporation of a finger guard, which kept the firer's finger from entering the ejection port.

In the lower front portion of the tubular outer barrel casing there were holes designed to help dissipate heat. These could also be used to affix a Sten sling, but when slung the Mk III would be carried upside down. Since British troops were trained to carry their submachine guns slung in the 'ready' position, sling-mounting cuts were made to the welded seam of the outer barrel casing to allow top sling mounting.

An experimental version of the Mk III, which relied heavily on stampings and pre-drilled holes. (Copyright Collector Grade Publications, Inc.)

The Mk III design was deemed ready for production, and Lines Brothers was awarded an initial contract for 500,000 of the Mk III Sten in January 1942. To meet this demand Lines Brothers operated 24 hours a day with three shifts, many workers being women who had been hired and trained to do gas- or spot-welding. Multiple production lines were set up so that if one had to be shut down for maintenance, Sten production continued. This initial order was completed in a year, as efficiency of design and production reduced manufacturing time to less than 5½ hours per Mk III. Even before the first contract was completed, Lines Brothers was awarded a contract for a further 500,000 Mk IIIs, although the contract was terminated after only 376,794 weapons were produced. A total of 876,794 Mk IIIs were produced, reportedly (although 876,886 was the official total. (Laidler 2000: 59).

The Mk III contained fewer parts than the Mk II (48 as opposed to 69), but most production savings were through faster, more efficient production methods. One potential problem that could arise if Mk II and Mk III Stens were issued to the same units was that for the most part, spare parts were not interchangeable. This was why the Mk II remained the primary submachine gun for front-line units. Unlike the Mk II, the Mk III had a magazine well that was welded in place and, hence, could not

A right-side view of the Mk III. This weapon has been cut away to illustrate the trigger mechanism. Note also that the seam along the top of the tube is visible, and that the brecch block is in the forward position. (REME Museum)

Australia's submachine guns – Owens and Austens

Although the rugged and reliable Owen submachine gun, initially in .22 calibre but eventually in 9mm calibre, was first demonstrated to the Australian military in July 1939 by its designer, 24-year-old Evelyn Owen, it was initially rejected as no use could be seen for such a weapon. The outbreak of war, however, convinced many in Australia that submachine guns were desirable and around 50,000 Owens were to be produced between 1941 and 1945. Japan's entry into the war in December 1941 confronted Australia with the very real possibility of invasion; previous estimates of the need for 10,000 'machine carbines' were quickly raised to 100,000. Another consideration was that the Owen had yet to be tested in combat, while the Sten had already seen service, and so production of the Sten commenced alongside the Owen. As there were no production facilities for 9mm ammunition in Australia, this issue had to be addressed as well; hence, a production line was set up at Footscray Ammunition Factory, Melbourne.

In March 1942 it was decided that Owens and Stens would each be produced at the rate of 500 per week. An order for 20,000 Australian-made Stens (which would come to be known as 'Austens') was given for joint production by Diecasters Pty Ltd of Melbourne and W.T. Carmichael and Sons Ltd of Sydney. The Austens were based on the Mk II, though a redesign so that diecasting could be used in its production would cause problems that caused it to fail its initial tests.

Among changes to the Austen was incorporation of a folding butt stock similar to that of the German MP 38. The Austen's stock was heavier than a typical Mk II stock and it required 20 parts (as

BELOW Officers and signallers struggle to keep dry at a 29th/46th Battalion forward command post near Gusika, Papua New Guinea, in November 1943. The corporal (second from left) has an Australian-designed Austen. Despite senior decision-makers' initial preference for it, the Austen was soon outperformed by the superior Owen, and was rarely used in combat. (AWM 016297)

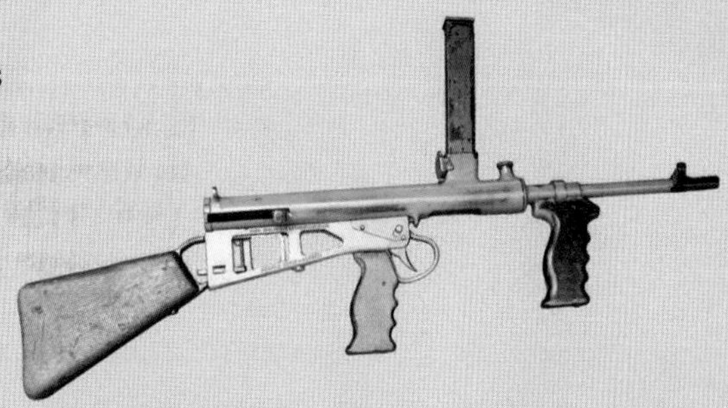

ABOVE The Australian Owen gun was rated superior to the Patchett/Sterling during UK trials and was considered far superior to the Austen, the Australian version of the Sten. (Author)

opposed to the two pieces of stamped steel required for the No. 3 stock)! Additonally, the stock was elongated to fit over the front pistol grip thus making it unwieldy when folded. This made length of pull uncomfortable for troops with short arms and made it difficult to get a good cheek weld when firing – so much for simplicity and ease of production. An increase in complexity was also apparent in the Austen's breech block and return spring, which required 16 parts as opposed to the Sten's 11. As the striker and firing pin were not integral they could become mixed up with those from other guns during any type of group cleaning, thus rendering many Austens unreliable. The fix was to number the striker and firing pin to the gun, but keeping the Sten's fixed firing pin would have been simpler. Once again, the striker and firing-pin system was based on the MP 38. Even the Austen magazine required more parts than the standard Sten magazine – 12, including two washers and two rivets not needed on the Sten, as opposed to eight – yet it held fewer rounds (28 rather than 32). Although some Sten parts were interchangeable with the Austen, others were not. Since British Stens were normally not used in the Australian Army during World War II this did not present an immediate problem.

Production of the diecast Austen was proving problematical as well. By January 1943, over 16,000 Owens had been delivered while only about 2,100 Austens had reached troops. By August 1944, the Austen was withdrawn from service and replaced by the Owen. Only 19,914 Austens had been produced.

At least some Austens were fitted with the suppressor as used on the Mk II (S) and did see some use with Australian troops, though this model was not introduced as the Austen Mk I (S) until August 1946. In an attempt to salvage the Austen, the manufacturers introduced a Mk II version, which used even more diecastings, but it was never adopted for service and only about 200 were produced. Though the Austens withdrawn during the war were kept in service for the Volunteer Defence Corps, Australia's equivalent to the Home Guard, after the war it was completely withdrawn with most being destroyed during the 1960s.

be rotated. As a result, it was less desirable for use by airborne troops. Nor could Mk III barrels be removed, which in addition to preventing disassembly for parachute drops, made them harder to clean. It also meant that if the Mk III's barrel was damaged, the weapon had to be scrapped for parts. However, even though the Mk II could be stowed more easily in a drop container than the Mk III, a substantial number of Mk IIIs were still dropped to Resistance groups in occupied Europe.

During 1943, consideration was given to ceasing production of the Mk II in favour of the Mk III, but the fact that Sten Mk II production was still outpacing Mk III production – and that more production defects were being reported in Mk IIIs than Mk IIs – prompted the decision to continue production of the Mk II; in fact, Mk III production was discontinued in September 1943 but production of the Mk II carried on.

As Mk III Stens were issued to the Home Guard in substantial numbers, the manual *Sten Carbine 9mm. Mk. II and Mk. III* devotes a section to the improvements incorporated into the Mk III. Its comments are concise but summarize the Mk III quite well:

> This model embodies a number of improvements designed chiefly to facilitate handling.
>
> 1. The weight of the Carbine is reduced to 6 lbs. 8 ozs. [the Mk II was 6lb 10oz]. The length (overall) is unaltered.
> 2. The barrel is not detachable and the barrel locking nut and catch are replaced by a barrel cover (or jacket) extending to within 1" of the muzzle. This provides a much improved forehand grip and a projection, immediately in front of the ejection opening, removes the danger of fingers being inadvertently placed through this opening.
> 3. The foresight of blade pattern is set on the front end of the barrel cover thus lengthening the sight base to 16 ½".
> 4. The trigger mechanism cover is now sprung on and off and the screws are no longer needed.
> 5. The internal mechanism is unaltered.
> 6. The change lever is now more certain and effective in its movement of the trip lever.
> 7. Cleaning of Barrel. As the barrel is not detachable, the breech block should be removed and the pullthrough drawn through from breech to muzzle. (Anonymous 1942b: 8)

THE STEN Mk IV

The term 'Sten Mk IV' was actually used for various experimental models. One version was developed from the Mk II for airborne troops; it was more compact and incorporated a folding stock. Another airborne version, the Mk IV Type A, had a curved wooden pistol grip at the rear of the receiver and an enlarged trigger guard, which would allow use

The Mk IV incorporated an array of experimental features: the barrel was shortened and featured a conical flash suppressor; the trigger mechanism was moved forward; it had a larger triggerguard to allow firing while wearing gloves in cold climates; and it featured a folding stock. It was only built as an experimental design. (Copyright Collector Grade Publications, Inc.)

while wearing gloves or mittens. Overall length was 27.5in and just 17.5in with the stock folded (the Mk II was 35.25in in length). Another, the Mk IV Type B, had a straight pistol grip located further forward and a smaller trigger guard. Both types had 3.85in-long barrels and conical flash suppressors. At least one prototype suppressed Mk IV Type A (S) was produced. A major factor in the two Mk IV types not entering service was the success of the subsequent Mk V Sten with airborne troops.

THE STEN Mk V

This next production Sten, therefore, was designated the Mk V. Testing of the Mk V, which retained many features of the Mk II, took place in January 1944. Included in the tests and evaluation were: interchangeability of parts with the Mk II Sten; 100yd and 200yd accuracy; reliability with an array of ammunition and when fired at various angles; endurance

New Zealand Stens

New Zealand had received two Sten samples and a set of production drawings by March 1942. It appears that the first drawings sent were for the Mk I, though a set of Mk II drawings were later acquired. As with Australia, there were no production facilities in New Zealand for 9mm ammunition. Though setting up a production line was considered, enough 9mm ammunition was imported from Australia, the USA and the UK that this was not deemed necessary.

The Royal New Zealand Air Force placed an order for 1,000 locally produced Mk II Stens for base defence. Barrels were not available in New Zealand but worn-out .303in rifle or machine-gun barrels could be cut to form three 7in Sten barrels, which could then be re-bored and re-rifled. The barrel problem solved, the RNZAF order was given to the Precision Engineering Company of Wellington, which completed the 1,000 Stens by the end of May 1942. Though identical to a British Mk II Sten, these guns were designated 'ARMAF Mk I'.

Though there had been consideration given to ordering Austens (see box on page 23), instead, a New Zealand Army order for 10,000 Stens followed, but due to a scarcity of worn-out .303in barrels, barrels had to be ordered from Australia. Unlike the ARMAF Mk I, the version produced for the New Zealand Army by The Radio Corporation of New Zealand in Wellington was not an exact copy of the Mk II but was instead a composite of the Mk II and Mk III, as it used a punched and welded tube with an integral magazine housing as did the Mk III, but with other features including a Mk II-type barrel and barrel nut. This version is designated the 'LP' (Local Production) model. An order for a further 5,000 'LP' Stens was generated in October 1943, but reportedly the order was never entirely fulfilled. In April 1949, the Stens produced in New Zealand were phased out within the New Zealand Armed Forces and replaced by the British-made Mk V Sten.

during a 10,000-round firing test; and penetration into 1in boards. During the endurance tests, problems arose due to improper case hardening of the breech blocks and sears.

A small run of the Mk V was produced at RSAF Enfield, likely to have been the experimental and trials weapons. Actual production, however, began on 1 February 1944 and continued until May 1945, with a total of 169,823 Mk Vs being produced at ROF Theale and 367,605 being made at ROF Fazakerley.

Many aficionados consider the Mk V the best Sten ever produced. Among its features were: front and rear pistol grips; detachable wooden stock with a rifle-type butt plate; a black barrel band mounting a front sight taken from the No. 4 Mk I rifle; two bayonet lugs; a black phosphate finish more durable than the previous finish, which was a type of bluing designated 'chemically stained'; a cocking handle that could be locked forward by pushing in and unlocked by pulling out; and a stud-and-flange seating system for the barrel to allow consistent alignment of the bore. The Mk V would take either of two standard British bayonets – the No. 7 Mk I or the No. 4 Mk II spike bayonet. (Note, also, that at least some Mk II Stens were equipped with a bayonet lug. The only bayonet standardized for the Mk II Sten was the Mk I spike bayonet; 75,800 of them were assembled during the war by Grundy Ltd of Toddington, Lines Brothers of Merton and N.J. Edwards Ltd of Sutton (Laidler 2000: 341).)

The front pistol grip was declared obsolete on 1 June 1945 because of a tendency for it to loosen owing to recoil and because force applied on the grip caused the barrel nut to move against the barrel nut catch thus causing failure properly to retain the barrel nut. However, it was popular with troops engaged in street fighting during the drive into Germany as it allowed them to shoot quickly from the hip. Note, too, that the Mk V trigger mechanism, though the same as that on the Mk II, was moved forward 1.3in so the rear pistol grip could be installed.

The Mk V was definitely of higher quality than its predecessors, but it also required more production time – at 12 man-hours per gun, more than twice that needed to turn out a Mk III. Cost was, likewise, substantially more. Thomas B. Nelson quotes the price, based on a Canadian Ordnance catalogue, of a Mk II or Mk III at US$10.99, and the cost of producing a Mk V at US$19.81 (Nelson 1977: 490). Although parts were interchangeable among Mk Vs, armourers soon found that as barrels were

This Mk V was manufactured after June 1945, when the addition of the front pistol grip was discontinued. (REME Museum)

zeroed to the rear sights of each weapon, it was necessary to stamp the serial number of the carbine onto the barrel to assure proper match-up. This would be especially necessary if units carried out group cleaning of weapons.

Sten accessories

For the most part, British and Commonwealth troops – including those equipped with Stens – wore 1937-pattern web equipment, although some were initially issued previous designs, such as the 1908 pattern, and a few troops received the stop-gap leather 1939 pattern during training (Chappell 2000: 13–21, 23–24, 33–35). The 1937 pattern, made from woven cotton webbing, became a 'universal' set (intended for all personnel regardless of weaponry) until the 1944 pattern, lighter but less durable, supplanted it in the Far East, seeing service in Korea, Malaya and Kenya. The 1937 and 1944 patterns were both designed with the Bren light machine gun in mind; each of the two rectangular pouches could hold two Bren magazines, but the pouches could not be fastened when filled with Sten magazines (Brayley 2001: 43); the Australians developed a larger pouch, standard issue from 1944, specifically to accommodate the 32-round Owen magazine (see page 23; Johnston 2007: 61–63).

Some Commandos and assault infantry on D-Day, though, wore the 1942 Battle Jerkin (Chappell 2000: 21–23), which could hold up to 12 Thompson or ten Sten magazines; the Battle Jerkin fell out of favour after June 1944, however.

Among the accessories for the Sten were two types of bandolier, each of which held seven magazines. The earlier pattern was designed to be worn across the chest, while the later pattern could be worn across the chest or at the waist. First priority to receive the bandoliers were airborne troops and Commandos. Airborne troops who carried extra ammunition were, of course, adding to an already heavy personal load; in the preparations for Operation *Market Garden* (see pages 38–44) Maj Michael Forman, OC B Company of the glider-borne 7th Battalion, The King's Own Scottish Borderers, made his men leave behind all the extra ammunition they had stowed as it would have overloaded their glider (Middlebrook 1994: 78).

To aid in loading Sten magazines, a process that could become difficult for the last few rounds, four different marques of loader were developed as World War II progressed. Of these only two – the Mk II (BE 8322) and the Mk IV (BE 8323) – really made it into general issue.

The Mk I Sten took a 46in rifle sling (AA 1657) but later slings were developed especially for the weapon; at first there was a 36in non-adjustable model (BE 8574), which was later supplanted by the adjustable Mk II (BE 8504), issued with the Mk V. Other accessories included a ruptured case extractor, a hooked L-shaped cleaning rod, and a parachutist's leg bag that fastened to the jumper's leg until released on a tether strap prior to landing, among others.

There were also Sten bayonets. For the Mk II Sten, a bayonet was developed reportedly at the request of Lord Lovat, the Commando officer who won a Distinguished Service Order at Dieppe, for use by the Commandos. A spike bayonet – 'Bayonet, Sten 9mm M/C, Mk1' – was developed and 75,800 were produced. The standard rifle spike bayonet – the No. 4 Mk II (BI/BA 6260), with a blade length of 9.875in – was the authorised bayonet for use with the Mk V Sten, but an innovative knife bayonet designated the No. 9 Mk I also saw extensive use on the Mk V after World War II.

At the end of World War II, as the size of the British Army decreased, a 'Storage and Transit Box' was developed for the Mk V Sten for weapons not immediately needed for issue. This box held one Mk V Sten, one sling, one Mk IV magazine loading tool, eight Mk II Sten magazines, one bayonet, one bayonet scabbard and one cleaning kit.

ABOVE A left-side view of the Mk III with Mk II sling fitted. (Courtesy of Rock Island Auction Galleries)

SUPPRESSED STENS

Early in the Sten's development, the Commandos, while retaining the Thompson as their standard-issue submachine gun throughout World War II, requested a suppressed (silenced) version of the Sten for use on raids. Requests also came in later from European Resistance groups. After trials of four suppressed variants of the Sten in November 1942, other prototype suppressed Stens were tested, and a model designated 'Carbine, m/c Sten, 9mm Mk2(S)' was eventually adopted. Note that the 'S' does not stand for 'silenced' or 'suppressed' but for 'Special Purpose'. Not 'officially' introduced until April 1945, the Mk II (S) was declared obsolescent at the same time. It had, however, seen some combat use from 1943 prior to its 'official' introduction. In fact, the Germans had captured some Mk II (S) Stens and designated them MP 751 (e).

The Mk II (S) was developed using a drilled barrel, which was surrounded by a jacket that extended past the muzzle. Baffles around the barrel helped dissipate the gases as they escaped from the barrel, while additional baffles in front of the muzzle helped dissipate remaining gases as they left the barrel. A muzzle plug sealed the opening in the double jacket and prevented gases from escaping as well as keeping the baffles in place. To prevent burns to the user's hand as the barrel became heated by the escaping gases, a canvas sleeve surrounded the barrel's jacket. The bolt was lightened and a couple of coils were removed from the recoil spring as well, to allow reliable operation with subsonic ammunition. The rear peep sight of the Sten Mk II (S) was reduced from a 200yd to a 100yd zero. In addition to the Commandos, the Special Operations Executive (SOE) and Resistance groups used the Mk II (S). SOE versions were designed so that the selector could only be set on semi-auto. Although it was strongly recommended that other suppressed Stens only be fired on semi-auto, they could be fired on full auto; however, a 30-round burst would burn out the suppressor, requiring a substantial amount of work by an armourer to replace the baffles.

The Mk II (S) performed well enough that it was decided to develop a suppressed version of the Mk V. Consideration was given to developing a suppressor that could be affixed to all marques of the Sten; however, the differences in front sight made this virtually impossible. Some Mk V Stens – reportedly about two dozen – were then converted to Mk V (S) configuration. The use of the anti-rotation peg designed to position the Mk V's barrel correctly, however, prevented use of the Mk II (S) type of barrel assembly. A 'fix' was developed by deleting the peg and machining a dovetail slot for the Mk II foresight, which could be fitted to the Mk V body casing to allow use of the Mk II (S) type of suppressor. After

This suppressed Mk II (S) was produced for SOE; note that it has the slanted 'T' grip characteristic of the Mk III. Because of the weight and length added by the suppressor, agents were trained for close-quarters use to place the stock under the armpit and lean well into the gun for more instinctive use. (Copyright Collector Grade Publications, Inc.)

Shooting around corners

Since the Sten Mk V remained in service after World War II, various experimental models can be traced to the 1950s. Among the most interesting was an example with a foregrip and butt, which could be swivelled to allow the Sten to be fired around corners or over the tops of barricades. It was also equipped with a 'prismatic' sight. Of course, British weapons designers would have been familiar with the German StG 44 assault rifle, with *Krumlauf* bent-barrel attachment designed to fire around corners and other experiments to develop this type of weapon. Middle Eastern house-to-house fighting has generated interest in such a design once again in the 21st century in weapons such as the Israeli 'Corner Shot' or the AimPoint CEU (Concealed Engagement Unit) designed for use with the CompM4 on the M4 Carbine or other weapons. An interesting sidenote is that India's National Security Guards counterterrorist unit added Corner Shot devices to its armoury after the Mumbai hotel sieges of 2008.

ABOVE An experimental Mk V, which incorporated a swivel butt and forward grip to allow firing around corners using its prismatic sight. (Copyright Collector Grade Publications, Inc.)

experimenting with the Mk V (S) guns, a purpose-built suppressed Sten, the Mk VI, was introduced.

Not counting those suppressed Stens produced for SOE and other special-operations usage, Laidler gives production figures for the Mk II (S) as a total of 5,776 and for the Mk VI as 24,824. ROF Theale and ROF Fazakarley produced Mk II (S) guns but only ROF Theale produced Mk VIs. The suppressor for the Mk VI was usable on Mk II (S) guns as well, which resulted in the Mk II (S) type of suppressor being declared obsolescent. Armourers found, however, that unlike the Mk II (S) suppressor, the Mk VI suppressor was much more difficult to disassemble for servicing.

Thomas B. Nelson gives total Sten production of all types as 3,750,000 and total magazines produced as 34,000,000 (Nelson 1977: 489). However, this figure is probably low; total production was actually over 4,000,000 and possibly over 4,500,000. Sources vary concerning total production by as much at 500,000. In the mid-1950s Stens in British (and Australian) service were reclassified. The Mk II became the L50 (where 'L' stands for Land Service), the Mk III was called the L51 and the Mk V became the L52. Mk II (S) and Mk VI Stens remained in British military service until the early 1970s, by which point they were replaced by the Sterling L34A1.

This suppressed Mk VI (S) has a pistol grip only. The magazine housing has been rotated downwards. Note the canvas sleeve added to the barrel to protect the shooter's hand from the heat generated by escaping gases. (REME Museum)

USE

The machine carbine in combat

The wartime manual *The Sten Machine Carbine* offers a concise general description of the Sten for World War II troops:

> The Sten Machine Carbine is a small and compact automatic weapon, it is a British invention, and can be likened to the Thompson Machine Carbine in many respects.
>
> It has, however, neither the finish nor the complicated mechanism of the Thompson Machine Carbine.
>
> It is simple to produce, there is little about it that can go wrong, and it is very simple in operation. In spite of this, it is very hardy and will stand up to a good deal of usage.
>
> A change lever is incorporated in the mechanism, permitting the carbine to be fired in single shots or bursts of fire.
>
> There is no cooling device on this weapon, but it is capable of firing from between eight and ten magazines in continuous bursts before getting too hot to hold. At this stage, dipping in water will effect the necessary cooling.
>
> The Mark I or Mark II model can be packed in a very small space by the removal of the butt and barrel and the rotation of the magazine housing to a downward position.
>
> The carbine is of the blowback type; thus when a round is fired the breech block is forced to the rear position by a portion of the explosive force.
>
> An interesting feature of this weapon is its fixed firing pin. (Anon n.d.: 5)

This offers a good layman's introductory summary of the Sten for contemporary users; however, the writer of the manual seems to have confused the ability of the Mk II to be disassembled for easy stowage with the Mk I, which did not lend itself to removal of the barrel nor have the rotating magazine housing.

The Sten Mk II loading tool. (Author)

HOME GUARD USE

A major challenge facing British military planners in 1940 was how to arm the men of the Local Defence Volunteers (on 22 July 1940 renamed the Home Guard at Churchill's insistence). The members of the Home Guard were initially issued the Thompson; in fact, they received it before the British Expeditionary Force.

Many in the Home Guard – particularly, one would assume, those who had handled the high-quality SMLE bolt-action rifle during World War I – were dismayed to receive the Sten, a comparatively crude weapon. 'They were said to cost thirty shillings each and I do not doubt it ... It is inaccurate over fifty yards and apt to be dangerous in the hands of an untrained man,' opined one Home Guard officer, while another Home Guard member believed the Sten's 'breeding might be described as by Woolworth out of Scrap Heap ... It works ... I am told, after being thrown into a river and dragged through mud' (Longmate 1974: 75). Even so, the September 1942 manual intended for the Home Guard, *Sten Carbine 9mm. Mk.II and Mk.III*, lauds the Mk II:

Sgt Bill Davies (right, with Mk II) leads his Home Guard platoon at Gresford Colliery in Wales, 15 April 1943. (IWM H 29023)

Submachine guns in use, 1939–41: a comparison

Although the British military authorities had resisted the submachine gun for two decades, the position changed abruptly in December 1939, when urgent requests were made for quantities of submachine guns for the British Expeditionary Force in France. This request may have been influenced by British observation of French practice; although only small numbers of the high-quality but rather underpowered 7.65mm MAS modèle 38 were available as the weapon had only entered production in 1939, submachine guns of various types were occasionally carried by *groupes francs*. Composed of volunteers from their parent unit, these small units of platoon strength undertook patrolling and raiding operations, a practice that began during World War I; as well as MAS-38s, the groupes francs also carried 9mm Erma EMP-35s, 3,250 of which had been seized from Spanish Republican soldiers fleeing across the Pyrenees, and Thompsons (Sumner & Vauvillier 1998a: 36 & 41).

German practice, influenced by the Condor Legion's involvement in the Spanish Civil War and the 1939 Polish campaign, may have also played a part in the change in British thinking. By the spring of 1940 most German infantry platoon commanders carried the 9mm MP 38 submachine gun, which had performed well in urban fighting in Poland, and in motorised, airborne and armoured units the weapon was regularly carried by NCOs as well.

As already noted, the Finnish Suomi submachine gun had made an excellent impression on British military planners; Finnish 'Motti' envelopment tactics, in which mobile Finnish strike teams armed with submachine guns and grenades would infiltrate into enemy lines and defeat their bogged-down Soviet opponents in detail, may have also influenced British decision-making concerning submachine guns (Jowett & Snodgrass 2006: 43–44).

The Italian armed forces had the reliable and accurate 9mm Beretta Modello 38A, but this popular and well-made weapon rarely found its way into the hands of line infantry units, and was expensive to manufacture. The US Navy and US Marine Corps purchased the Model 1928 and M1928A1 Thompson in large numbers throughout the 1930s, and the Thompson was adopted by the US Army in 1938; even so, the Thompson was normally reserved for tank crews, Rangers and other specialists. From 1940, the Japanese had small numbers of the 8mm Type 100, based on the MP 28/II, but, as with the Italians, none reached regular infantry units.

BELOW Finnish recruits train with Suomi submachine guns with 71-round drum magazines while their instructor and fellow trainees look on. The kp/31 was a very well-made weapon which operated efficiently in the extreme conditions faced in Finland, though it was expensive to manufacture. The officer with his hands on his hips appears to be from the Civil Guard. Experienced Civil Guardsmen were often responsible for this kind of training on behalf of the regular Army. (ADEQHA)

> The Home Guard will realise that its fire power has been considerably increased by the introduction of this, its latest weapon. The most effective use of the Sten Carbine can only be secured by constant handling. This applies to the operation of the cocking handle and change lever, charging and changing magazines and unloading, and also the quick and automatic alignment of sights from the shoulder and from the hip. A firm grip with both hands is essential.
>
> Waste no time – read the following and become familiar with the construction, handling, care and uses of the Sten. (Anon 1942b: 2)

The manual goes on to offer a concise explanation of the weapon:

> The Sten Machine Carbine Mk II, 9mm. will fire all types of 9mm. round nose rimless ammunition. Some Machine Carbines of the German Army also use this type of ammunition. Operation is by blowback and return spring. Firing may be 'automatic' (in bursts) or 'Single Shots'. Carbine should be fired dry and thoroughly clean. Barrel and butt are easily detachable to facilitate carriage. Fixed sights for use up to 200 yds. (Anon 1942b: 2)

The most famous Home Guard user of the Sten was its Colonel-in-Chief, HM King George VI, who carried a Mk II in a custom-built wooden briefcase and had a range built in the Buckingham Palace gardens so he could practise with it.

The first issue of Mk III Stens was in April 1942 to the men of the Home Guard, who had turned in their Thompsons so that they could be issued to the Commandos. (Initially, those members of the Army not issued rifles were issued with Mk II Stens, such as NCOs and those in support functions, while the Home Guard got the Mk III Stens. Once the Home Guard was fully equipped, then Mk III Stens were also issued to Army units.)

This particular Mk II was issued to HM King George VI, in his capacity as a member of the Home Guard. The gun's unusually high standard of finish indicates that it was especially prepared for the King. Associated with it is a hand-built wooden case, which also accommodates spare magazines and a magazine loader. (IWM FIR 6283)

Along with the Home Guard, the highly secret Auxiliary Units, specially trained to act as stay-behind guerrilla fighters should Great Britain be invaded by the Germans, were also issued Stens; they had received M1928 Thompsons in spring 1940, ahead of Regular Army units. Interestingly, some members of the Auxiliary Units compared the Sten favourably with the Thompson: 'Exaggerated reports about unreliability [of the Sten] were usually related to the quality of manufacture. Don Handscombe and his comrades in the Thundersley Patrol of the Auxiliary Units rated them more reliable than the Thompson SMG' (Warwicker 2008: 130).

AIRBORNE USE

The developmental history of the Sten was shaped by the requirements of Britain's fledgling airborne forces; a light, cheap weapon, devastating at close quarters, that could be dismantled for parachute jumps and could use enemy ammunition, the Sten appeared to fulfil many of the new arm's requirements. Exactly what percentage of the armament that British airborne forces normally carried in combat was composed of Stens is open to some discussion, however. A parachute battalion, *c.*1942/43, had an authorized total strength of 613 personnel, significantly lower than the standard infantry battalion (around 800). In 1942, the 'pool reserve' for the parachute battalion showed 429 Stens, presumably Mk IIs at this time. However, it is quite unlikely that more than half the battalion carried Stens unless anticipating urban combat, and that rifles continued to be used in substantial numbers, forming standard issue for most British airborne troops throughout World War II. The air-landing battalion establishment of 864 all ranks was much closer to the standard infantry battalion strength.[2]

In *The Red Beret*, Hilary St George Saunders describes the initial issue of Mk IIs to British airborne troops of C Company, 2nd Parachute Battalion participating in Operation *Biting*, the 27–28 February 1942 raid to capture German radar equipment at Bruneval. C Company was commanded by Maj John Frost, who went on to command 2nd Parachute Battalion. The Bruneval raid was only the second operation in which Britain's fledgling airborne forces played a part:

> As the winter days went by Captain J.G. Ross, a Scotsman from Dundee, and Frost's second-in-command, began to receive an ever-increasing quantity of stores. These arrived at irregular intervals, both by day and by night. Soon every man was equipped with the then newly invented Sten gun, something between an automatic rifle and an automatic pistol. At the time it had not been perfected – as the Canadians were to find to their cost some months later at Dieppe [see page 45] – and therefore contained a number of defects absent from the later model. These the parachute troops did their best to discover and remedy, being consoled

[2] I am grateful to Gary Kennedy for the useful statistics on airborne manpower compiled on his website <www.bayonetstrength.150m.com>

> by the fact that, though the new weapon might not be perfect, it was greatly superior up to a range of fifty yards to the rifle and bayonet to which they had up till then been equipped. (Saunders 1952: 59)

Airborne troops soon discovered problems with the Sten's rudimentary safety when it was carried on jumps in North Africa. On 12 November 1942, 3rd Parachute Battalion, fresh from England, made the British Army's first battalion-sized operational parachute jump, to seize an airfield at Bône on the Tunisia–Algeria border. The only airborne soldier to die in the jump tragically shot himself with his own Sten during the descent. On 16 November, 1st Parachute Battalion jumped at Souk el Arba, about 90 miles west of Tunis, with orders to capture and hold Béja, an important road junction, in advance of First Army. One parachutist was strangled when a rigging line became entangled around his neck, and four others were wounded by a Sten that accidentally discharged. Of the two men killed and 19 injured in these two jumps, the Germans accounted for none, but the Sten had accounted for five (Harclerode 1992: 32–33).

The 'pathfinders' of 21st Independent Parachute Company were trained to drop ahead of the main body of troops and tasked with marking the dropping and landing zones (Middlebrook 1994: 33). Occasionally, however, they found themselves in the conventional infantry role. In *First In*, his book about his time with 21st Independent Parachute Company, Ron Kent relates an incident in September 1943, following the amphibious landings in mainland Italy, in which the Sten proved more dangerous to its users than the enemy:

This airborne soldier is carrying his Mk II in pieces – stock, receiver and barrel, and magazine – strapped to his chest. This ability to disassemble the Mk II for use by parachute troops was one reason it replaced the Mk I. (IWM TR 57)

> In all this advance the Company suffered no more casualties, other than one that was due, not to enemy action, but to the instability of the old model Sten [probably the Mk II]. Sid Humphries sustained a nasty nick below the knee cap when his section sergeant, rounding some rocks, accidentally caught the toe of his boot against the butt of a Sten leaning against a stone and pointing straight at where Sid was busy cooking for his section. The miserable weapon fired a 9 millimetre bullet at Sid's leg. Sid's reaction was quite calm. He just stood there looking surprised and amazed at his sergeant as if to say 'I'm not that bad a cook, am I?' Some speedy first aid from 'Doc' Toms and a day or two's rest of the leg and a few more days of stiff leggedness and Sid was back in action again. (Kent 1979: 66–67)

The soldiers of 1st Airborne Division had played a crucial role in operations in Sicily and Italy during 1943, but in June 1944 it was 6th Airborne Division that spearheaded the British and Canadian D-Day invasion effort in Normandy. Specially formed for the invasion, 6th Airborne Division was tasked with seizing and holding bridges over the Orne river and canal, and destroying the heavy coastal battery at Merville and the bridges over the River Dives.

By June 1944, the establishment of an airborne division comprised 12,416 officers and men, armed with 6,504 Stens; for comparison, 7,171 rifles were issued (Bouchery 2001: 23). The realization that a substantial number of airborne soldiers would still carry rifles seems to be reflected in the 1944/45 parachute battalion 'pool reserve', which at that point only included 300 Stens (the total strength remained 613 all ranks). Glider-borne battalions seem to have been issued a higher proportion of rifles as troops did not have to jump with their weapons. During the 1943–45 period, Stens were issued to rifle-platoon commanders and their batmen and rifle-section commanders, as well as signallers, pioneers and some other troops of the glider-borne battalions.[3]

The glider-borne soldiers of B and D Companies, 2nd Battalion, The Oxfordshire and Buckinghamshire Light Infantry, carried Mk V Stens into battle in Normandy alongside the usual complement of rifles and Bren guns. Their job was to seize and hold the vital Orne river and canal bridges. Lt Richard 'Sandy' Smith, OC No. 14 Platoon, nursing a knee injury, was leading his men at the hobble over Bénouville Bridge (later renamed Pegasus Bridge) when a German threw a grenade at him: 'I was very lucky. I don't really know what happened. I just felt this smack. I didn't see him throw the stick grenade. I saw him climbing over the wall to get to the other side and I shot him as he was going over – I made certain too. I gave him quite a lot of rounds, firing from the hip – it was very close range' (Fowler 2010: 39). Lt Smith received the Military Cross for his part in this successful action.

Those parachuting into Normandy found that problems with the Sten persisted; as the men of 8th Parachute Battalion landed at their drop zone near Troarn, the CO, Lt Col Alastair Pearson, was shot in the hand when a soldier's Sten gun went off accidentally. Lt Ellis 'Dixie' Dean of 13th Parachute Battalion made a tree landing and relates the problem caused by carrying the Sten disassembled and tucked into his parachute harness:

A close-up of the Mk II's selector. When it is pushed through to the right (as shown here), it is on semi-automatic mode; when it is pushed through to the left, it is on full-automatic mode. (Author)

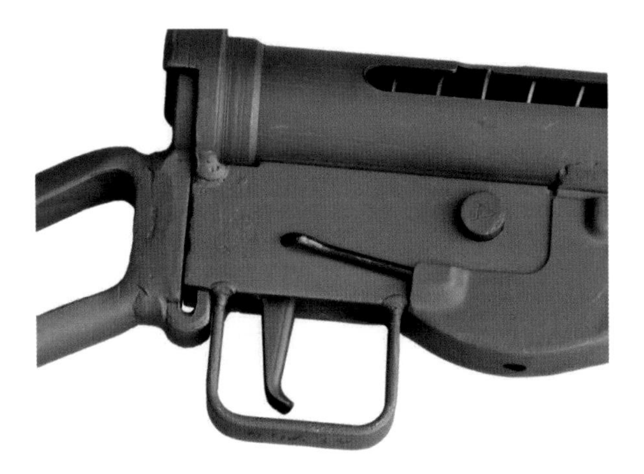

> Down I came, crashing through branches and foliage without so much as a scratch or bruise, but when I stopped falling and opened my eyes, I was completely enclosed by greenery. I felt around for a branch to get my feet on, but found none, so I turned the quick release on the parachute harness, gave it a bang, the straps flew apart and my Sten, which was broken into three parts, and threaded under them, fell to the ground ... (Barber 2009: 119)

[3] See <www.bayonetstrength.150m.com>

In contrast, Pte John Butler of 7th Parachute Battalion landed with his Sten stowed in his leg bag. Those who landed in marshy ground found that their heavily laden leg bags sank into the mud, while in other cases the webbing attachment broke. Although his weapon survived the jump, Butler was not impressed with the 9mm Sten's seeming lack of stopping power once contact was made with the enemy:

Carrying, holding and firing the Sten

The August 1942 *Small Arms Training* pamphlet on the Sten, designed for instructors to use, highlights the value of the weapon: 'The weapon is especially useful when on patrol or for fighting in close country such as woods and villages. Under these conditions the enemy may appear at close ranges and from different directions, and by firing from the waist such targets can be instantly engaged. Where time permits the weapon will always be fired from the shoulder' (Anon 1942a: 3). The pamphlet goes on to explain the two optimal ways to hold the Sten:

1. *Holding*

i. Explain:–
Holding is of the first importance, especially when firing in bursts. Correct holding can be gained only by experience in firing ball ammunition.

ii. There are two positions for holding the machine carbine, viz.:
(a) At the waist.
(b) At the shoulder.

2. i. Explain and demonstrate:–
Holding at the waist. – The left foot is advanced with the knee bent, the weight of the body being balanced on the left foot. The right hand is on the butt with the forefinger on the trigger, the left hand on the barrel locking nut with the wrist under the magazine, the butt of the weapon is pressed tightly against the side into the body in order that, no matter in which direction the firer turns, the weapon is brought automatically in the same direction. The muzzle is directed towards the centre of target. Care must be taken that the little finger of the left hand is clear of the ejection opening. The attention of the firer must be concentrated on the target.

ii. Practise squad, instructor standing behind man and checking that the barrel is aligned on target.

3. i. Explain and demonstrate:–
Holding in the shoulder. – The position of the body and hands is the same as for holding at the waist. The right elbow is raised and the right shoulder pushed well forward into the butt. (Anon 1942a: 4–5)

The Small Arms Training pamphlet then deals with firing:

i. Owing to the speed with which single rounds can be fired, the greater accuracy obtained by this method and the need for economy of ammunition, single round firing will be employed whenever possible. Bursts should be reserved for extreme emergencies, and, when used, should be of 2 or 3 rounds only.

ii. The machine carbine can be carried in any convenient position but when expecting to meet the enemy it should be held at the waist. From this position it can be instantly cocked and fired, or, time permitting, it will be fired from the shoulder. Although the weapon can be fired whilst on the move, greater accuracy is obtained by halting momentarily to do so.

iii. For targets at about 25 yards the weapon may be fired from the waist by sense of direction. For ranges between 25 and 100 yards, and if time permits, aim will be taken using the battle sight. Whichever method is used an attempt should be made to observe the strike of the shots, as this is the only quick method of making necessary corrections. (Anon 1942a: 5–6)

ABOVE The Mk II's triangular front sight. This was a very rudimentary front sight but it could be acquired rapidly through the rear peep sight. The rifle-type sights on the Mk V were much more usable at longer ranges. (Author)

The men of the Polish 1st Independent Parachute Brigade fought at Arnhem equipped in much the same way as their British and Canadian equivalents. This Polish airborne soldier carries a Mk V. (Polish Institute and Sikorsky Museum)

I was kneeling back looking at the top of the slope with my Sten gun pointing. Suddenly, a Jerry came in view with his rifle pointing towards me and I pressed the trigger of my Sten, but to my horror the man didn't fall down as I expected and just stood looking at me, and I was in absolute terror. Then the magazine ran out, it had been about half full, twelve to fourteen rounds, and probably took about two to two and a half seconds to fire off. And then the man came at me, collapsing on top of me and his bayonet pierced my left thigh, hit the bone and flipped out again, and the left side of my smock was covered in blood.

Now all of this had taken but two or three seconds, though it seemed like minutes that the man was standing at the top of the bank leering at me. He was of course dead, and the thud of the bullets in his chest had held him for those few seconds, though at the time I did not realize this. (Barber 2009: 189)

The men of 6th Airborne Division went on to see 82 consecutive days of action in Normandy, taking about 20 per cent casualties and only being withdrawn on 27 August.

THE STEN AT ARNHEM

Although the Mk V had been in production since February 1944 and photographic evidence shows that some saw action in the struggle for Normandy in June–August 1944, the first troops to receive the Mk V in large numbers were members of 1st Airborne Division, who took it into action during Operation *Market Garden*, the audacious but flawed bid to seize the Rhine bridges in The Netherlands and hasten victory over Nazi Germany. As they had with the Mk II Sten, British airborne troops normally removed the butt of the Mk V during a jump and tucked the shortened weapon into their parachute harness across their chest.

Parachuting into battle entailed taking a formidable array of equipment. Maj Geoffrey Powell of 156th Parachute Battalion recalled the load he carried for his unit's *Market Garden* jump, on Sunday 17 September 1944:

A haversack containing maps, torch and other odds and ends; respirator, water-bottle and compass; pistol-holder and ammunition case; and on my chest the two pouches crammed with Sten magazines and hand grenades. Across my stomach I then tied my small pack, solid with two days' concentrated rations, mess tin, spare socks, washing kit, pullover, a tin mug, all topped with a Hawkins anti-tank grenade. Slung around my neck were binoculars, while a large shell dressing, a morphia syringe

Four British airborne soldiers move through a shell-damaged house in Oosterbeek to which they had retreated after being driven out of Arnhem in September 1944. Note the Mk V carried by the soldier in the left foreground. (Cody Images)

> and red beret were tucked into my smock pockets. Next I wrapped myself in a denim jumping-jacket to hold the bits and pieces in place and prevent the parachute cords snagging on the many protruberances. Over everything went a Mae West life-jacket with a camouflage net scarfed around my neck and the parachutist's steel helmet, covered with a scrim-decorated net, on my head. Onto my right leg I then tied a large bag, into which was packed a Sten gun, together with an oblong-shaped walkie-talkie radio, and a small entrenching tool; a quick release catch allowed this bag to be lowered in mid-air so that it would dangle below on a thin cord and hit the ground before I did … (Powell 1998: 20–21)

Based on at least some comments by airborne troops who jumped during *Market Garden*, the Mk V performed more reliably than had the Mk II. For example, Lt Jimmy Cleminson, OC No. 5 Platoon, B Company, 3rd Parachute Battalion, describes an encounter with a German armoured vehicle on Sunday 17 September, the first day of the operation:

> I realized that nobody had got their Gammon bombs prepared to chuck at armoured vehicles, as the sticks of plastic explosive were still firmly wedged in our back pockets. I got up into a house and found myself behind the German vehicle. I was joined by [Maj] Peter Waddy [OC B Company]. I shot a German soldier in the garden below me with my Sten and wondered what I could do to get rid of our armoured visitor. (Middlebrook 1994: 132)

What is noteworthy about his account is that there are no negative comments about the Sten or its performance as there often were in earlier narratives in which the Mk I or Mk II was being used. Cleminson went on to be wounded and captured, and was awarded the Military Cross.

Elements of 1st Airborne Division reached the Arnhem bridge and came under attack from armoured forces during Monday 18 September. Some men had already picked up German weapons, but Signalman Bill Jukes of 2nd Parachute Battalion appreciated the chance to use his Sten that morning:

> The first vehicle which drew level with the house was hit, and the second rammed into it, blocking the roadway. The rest didn't stand a chance. The crews and passengers, those still able to, began to pile out, and those of us armed with Stens joined in the general fusillade. One of the radio operators grabbed my Sten, which was leaning against the wall, but I snatched it away from him, telling him to go get his own. I hadn't waited five years to get a shot at the enemy like this only to be denied by some Johnny-come-lately to the section. It was impossible to say what effect my shooting had. There was such a volley coming from the windows along the street that nobody could have said who shot who ... (Middlebrook 1994: 294)

Sometimes the Sten didn't stand up to the shock of landing. The second drop was delayed by poor weather until the afternoon of Monday 18 September; Spr Arthur Ayers of 4th Parachute Squadron, Royal Engineers, was part of it, coming down near the Ede–Arnhem railway line. Ayers landed heavily, hitting his head on the ground; when he reached for his leg bag he found that the barrel of his Sten had been bent by the impact, and the weapon was useless (Nichol & Rennell 2011: 84).

Cpl David Jones of 156th Parachute Battalion, which also dropped on the afternoon of 18 September, mentions the advantages of the Sten's 9mm chambering:

> Then [soon after landing] we found a truck loaded with German ammunition and weapons. I realized that I had a prize here. Airborne troops were always short of vehicles and ammunition; our Stens were designed to use the German rimless 9-millimetre ammunition. I told the lads to jump on the truck and I had visions of driving off to the company RV with some transport and a load of ammunition ... I knew Major [John] Waddy [OC B Company, 156th Parachute Battalion, who usually carried a German MP 40] would be pleased ... (Middlebrook 1994: 240)

Unfortunately, before he could reach his company, Jones was ordered to unload the ammunition and assist with casualty evacuation.

Those men of the Royal Engineers who served with the airborne divisions were fully trained as infantry in addition to their specialist roles

The Mk V at Arnhem **(previous pages)**

On the sixth day of Operation *Market Garden*, Friday 22 September 1944, as the German cordon around the Oosterbeek pocket tightens, two members of the British 1st Airborne Division have ambushed two German Waffen-SS soldiers. The British sergeant is a pathfinder from 21st Independent Parachute Company. He is armed with a Sten Mk V. The 1st Airborne Division corporal is also armed with a Sten Mk V. Although some Mk Vs had been available for the D-Day jump, it was during the preparations for Operation *Market Garden* that the Mk V received wide issuance. Note that at this point, the front pistol grip is still used; on later versions of the Mk V (produced after June 1945) it would be removed.

This Mk V is fitted with a No. 4 bayonet. How often the Sten was used with a bayonet in combat is unclear, but at close quarters when ammunition is all expended the bayonet allowed the soldier to continue to fight. The intimidation factor would have made bayonets useful for Military Police or others controlling prisoners. (Copyright Collector Grade Publications, Inc.)

(Middlebrook 1994: 36). In the small hours of the morning of Tuesday 19 September, Maj Eric Mackay of 1st Parachute Squadron, Royal Engineers, was holed up with his men in a school house close to the bridge at Arnhem. Finding that the school was surrounded by about 60 German soldiers who were seemingly unaware of the British airborne troops only yards away from them, Mackay's men took up position, grenades at the ready: 'On a signal, they were dropped on the heads below, followed instantly by bursts from all our six Brens and fourteen Stens. Disdaining cover, the boys stood up on the window-sills, firing from the hip. The night dissolved into a hideous din as the heavy crash of the Brens mixed with the high-pitched rattle of the Stens, the cries of wounded men and the sharp explosions of grenades' (Nichol & Rennell 2011: 70).

Some, though, found their Stens failed them at the crucial moment. On Wednesday 20 September, as 4th Parachute Brigade sought to reach the Oosterbeek perimeter, Maj Powell was ordered to lead the 25 survivors of his C Company, 156th Parachute Battalion, in a charge on German forces located in a hollow alongside a road some 200yd away: 'No one hesitated. The men rose to their feet the moment I stepped out into the open ... I brought my Sten down to hip-level to press the trigger; it flashed through my mind that this was the first time I had fired the weapon since the battle started. My forefinger squeezed the metal. Nothing happened. It had jammed ...' (Powell 1998: 120–21). The Germans fled, and Powell later armed himself with a German submachine gun to replace his jammed Sten.

During the night of 20/21 September, as the surrounded British forces struggled to hold the Oosterbeek perimeter against repeated German attacks, Capt James Livingstone of the glider-borne 7th Battalion, The King's Own Scottish Borderers, found his Sten highly effective at close quarters:

> They came across running and shouting to within about 20 yards of us before I opened fire. I killed an awful lot of Germans then, with my Sten. There was a big tree in front of me, and there was one German who was on his knees, wounded, but still preparing to fire. I remember [Capt] David Clayhills, the Adjutant ... shouting 'Kill the bastard!', and I did so. I'm a bit ashamed of it now, but I was bloody angry at the time. (Middlebrook 1994: 347)

Many of those who took part in *Market Garden* were captured, including scores of wounded men. Pte Roland Atkinson of 156th Parachute Battalion, who had been shot in the neck, was captured at the main dressing station at the Schoonoord Hotel in Oosterbeek. He recalled seeing a Sten in German hands: 'A Tiger tank pulled up just outside, and out jumped an officer who proceeded to enter the dressing station with a vicious-looking bodyguard. He looked what the Germans would call a typical Nordic type – blond hair, blue eyes (a little bloodshot!) – and as he walked down between the rows of wounded he brandished a Sten gun…' (Middlebrook 1994: 382–83)

THE STEN IN THE MEDITERRANEAN

In *The Sten Machine Carbine* Peter Laidler quotes a 25 May 1942 report from a British officer, Capt Woodall, serving in the Western Desert:

> Lt. Col. Barlow and myself each had a Sten as our personal weapon in the desert. The two guns we had were toolroom models – a Mark I and a Mark II. We gave demonstrations whenever possible, using captured German ammunition for the most part. The guns both behaved perfectly throughout. The highlight of our demonstration was when we allowed one of the spectators to fill the breech completely with fine sand. This was then shaken out, a magazine inserted and the gun invariably fired. We occasionally had a bulged case [possibly because of increased pressure due to a partially obstructed bore] when doing this, but it had no effect on the functioning of the gun. One of the great advantages of this weapon is that it will function without any oil whatsoever. Another noticeable feature is the good grouping[4] which can be obtained when firing automatic. In every respect these Stens were superior to the Thompson, but again their value in open warfare is doubtful. (Laidler 2000: 47)

It may be presumed that the comment on the value of the Sten in 'open warfare' refers to its limited range, which in the desert would be an issue. Although the Sten's range might at times be given as 100yd or even 200yd for accurate aimed fire, 50yd would be more achievable for most users. It seems that Stens did not see widespread use in the Mediterranean except with airborne and possibly RAF personnel, with the weapon only appearing in significant numbers in Italy in the last year of the war (Brayley 2002a: 43).

A left-side view of a Mk II with magazine in place. The flat-black finish was good for combat as it was non-reflective. (Courtesy of Rock Island Auction Gallery)

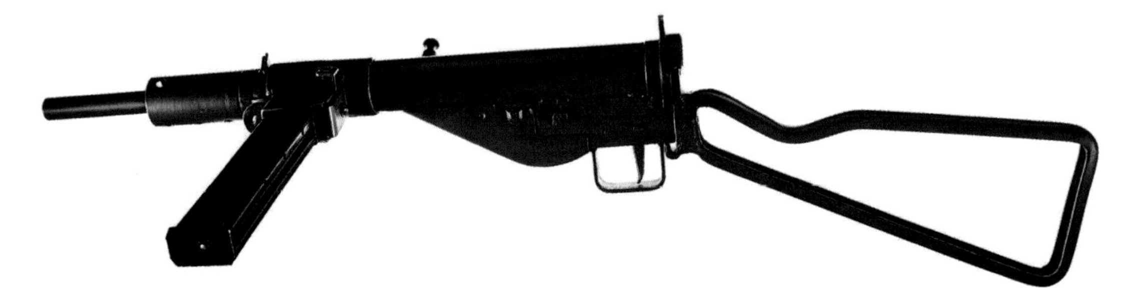

[4] 'Grouping' refers to how close together shots are when fired, an indication of accuracy

DIEPPE, D-DAY AND BEYOND

Among early users of the Sten were troops of Canadian 2nd Infantry Division, who reportedly were the first to use the Canadian-manufactured Mk II (Myatt 1981: 113) during the disastrous Dieppe raid of 19 August 1942. They were not impressed:

> One of the Canadian force's main complaints during the entire raid was the trouble they had with their Sten guns. The 9mm submachine guns were meant to give small units extra firepower in the same way that the Thompson did with the Commandos. But the guns were in short supply, and while some of the Canadians had trained with the Sten guns before Rutter [Operation *Rutter* was the previously planned 7 July 1942 raid on Dieppe, which was cancelled due to bad weather], the weapons had been returned when the raid was called off. New weapons were issued just before the raid; they came straight from storage and were well clogged with grease. There was no time to refine the guns, which had a tendency to jam easily; some Canadian soldiers had discovered during the rehearsals for Rutter that this could be fixed by adjustments to the firing mechanism and honing down the hammer. Major [A.T. 'Tony'] Law [who took charge of The Queen's Own Cameron Highlanders of Canada after the CO was killed during the landing] said later that no one in his regiment had actually had a chance to fire the weapon during rehearsals before the raid because of the shortage of ammunition. (Defelice 2008: 169)

The Dieppe raid gave the Allied planners many painful lessons that would be put to good use on D-Day. In the ensuing months Stens were widely issued to Commonwealth infantry units preparing for the opening of the 'Second Front', as well as those foreign troops – French, Polish and other nationalities – issued British clothing, weapons and equipment.

The 1944 D-Day landings – and the bitter, close-quarter fighting in the streets and hedgerows of Normandy that ensued – provided an abundance of just the sort of tactical situations the Sten was designed for. The Sten proved decisive in the hands of CSM Stanley Hollis of 6th Battalion, The Green Howards, during the battle to suppress the Mont Fleury Battery during the 6 June landings on Gold Beach. In Hollis's own words (two decades later):

The Mk V was far less 'austere' in construction than its predecessors; it featured front and rear pistol grips and a wooden butt. Quality control over the manufacturing process was more strictly applied. As a result a Mk V took about twice as many man-hours to manufacture as a Mk II. This change reflected Britain's improved position with regard to armaments by the time production of the Mk V commenced, in February 1944. The Mk V Sten was assembled at both ROF Theale in Berkshire and ROF Fazakerley in Lancashire. This gun is one of 169,823 Mk Vs made at ROF Theale. It is fitted with a forward pistol grip; this was subsequently deleted from production in June 1945. (IWM FIR 6340)

Stens in the British infantry battalion in North-West Europe, 1944–45

On the eve of D-Day, the British infantry battalion comprised 36 officers and 809 men, divided into four rifle companies, a support company, a headquarter company and the battalion headquarters. The battalion was issued 56 Stens (52 of these to the rifle companies), as opposed to 695 rifles (400 to the rifle companies) and 63 Bren guns (40 to the rifle companies). In practice, it is likely that many more Stens were carried, as the official figures assumed that only the 36 section commanders and 16 2in-mortar No. 1s of the rifle companies, plus only four more personnel in the other parts of the battalion, were armed with Stens. In fact, many rifle-company officers and some non-rifle-company personnel would have carried Stens.

At this time the British ten-man infantry section was (in theory) divided into a seven-man rifle group and a three-man Bren group. The section commander, a corporal, led the rifle group; he was armed with a Sten, and carried five 32-round magazines and two No. 36 Mills Bombs (grenades). Each of the six riflemen in the rifle group carried a .303in Lee-Enfield rifle, ten five-round magazine clips, two Bren-gun magazines (each containing 30 rounds) and one No. 36 Mills Bomb. A lance-corporal or experienced private led the Bren group; he was armed with a Lee-Enfield and carried ten five-round magazine clips and four Bren magazines. The Bren gunner (No. 1) carried the Bren gun plus four Bren magazines, while his No. 2 was armed with a Lee-Enfield and carried ten five-round magazine clips, five Bren magazines and two No. 36 Mills bombs (Bouchery 2001: 41–46).

> Major [Ronnie] Lofthouse [Hollis's company commander] said to me, 'There's a pillbox there Sergeant Major.' Well, when he said that I saw it, it was very well camouflaged and I saw these guns moving around in the slits and I got my Sten gun and I rushed at it, spraying it hosepipe fashion. They fired back at me and they missed. I don't know whether they were more panic-stricken than me, but they must have been. And I got on top of it and I threw a grenade through the slit, and it must have sickened them. I went round the back and went inside and there were two dead and quite a lot of prisoners. They were quite willing to forget all about the war. (Morgan 2004: 62)

Hollis then followed a trench that led him to a second bunker, and the Germans in it promptly surrendered; 'we found out later that this was the command post for the Mont Fleury gun battery, which was just over the brow of the hill' (Morgan 2004: 62). Together with further actions later that day, the success at the Mont Fleury Battery won Hollis the Victoria Cross, the only one to be awarded for a D-Day exploit.

The close-quarter fighting continued as the Allied forces pushed inland. Troops and tanks of 12th SS-Panzer Division counterattacked Canadian positions in Bretteville-l'Orgueilleuse on the evening of 8 June 1944. A passage from the account of the action given by Lt Col F.M. Matheson DSO, CO 1st Battalion, The Regina Rifles, is quoted in Volume III of the Canadian Army's official history of World War II. It demonstrates that even senior officers had reason to be armed with the Sten: 'Altogether 22 Panthers circled about [the Regina Rifles'] Battalion HQ and A Company's position during the night, and it is hard to picture the confusion which existed. Contact with all but D Company was lost. Fires and flares lit up the area, and the enemy several times appeared to be convinced that opposition had ceased. A foolhardy German despatch rider rode through Bretteville on a captured Canadian motorcycle, only to be brought down by the CO's Sten gun' (Stacey 1960: 137).

As the fighting in Normandy wore on, many Canadian NCOs and officers reportedly discarded their Stens and 1937-pattern pouches (see page 27) in favour of the .303in rifle and 50-round bandoliers; Maj (later Col) Jacques Ostiguy of Le Régiment le Maisonneuve, which had seen action at Dieppe and landed in Normandy one month after D-Day, observed that the Canadians' Stens were 'more dangerous to ourselves than to the Germans' (Chartrand 2001: 45). Another Canadian officer, Maj L.L. Dickin of 1st Battalion, The South Saskatchewan Regiment, reported an unorthodox use of the Sten in hand-to-hand combat: 'On one occasion my corporal pulled the trigger of his sten at the same time as the Nazi fired his rifle. Both triggers clicked, the sten was out of ammo and the German rifle jammed. So the corporal hit the Nazi over the head with his sten and then shot him with his own rifle after clearing the jammed bullet' (Tout 2000: 217)

A large and experienced contingent of Polish soldiers played a key role in the campaign to liberate Western Europe in the months following D-Day. Here we see two soldiers of the Polish 1st Armoured Division, one with a Mk III, during the fighting for Thielt, Belgium, on 8 September 1944. (Polish Institute and Sikorsky Museum)

The soldiers of XXX Corps, desperately trying to relieve the encircled airborne forces at Arnhem, also had reason to value their Stens. On Thursday 21 September, L/Cpl Denis Longmate of 4th Battalion, The Dorsetshire Regiment, survived crossing the Rhine in small boats, but his party was greatly reduced in numbers:

> Finally, there were just three of us left. It was still raining, all was quiet and there was no movement. And we were debating what we were going to do when a German patrol appeared, about a dozen men coming in our direction. 'Are we going to kill or be killed? It's them or us.' It was pretty poor odds with a dozen of them and three of us. But I told the other two to hold their fire and when the patrol came in range I fired the Sten. I'd never killed at such close quarters before, literally seeing the whites of the eyes. I saw the bullets hit, saw them go down, all of them. (Nichol & Rennell 2011: 219)

The advance towards Germany in the autumn of 1944 thrust many who were ill-prepared for combat into the front line. Capt George Blackburn of 4th Field Regiment, Royal Canadian Artillery, recalled an incident involving the Sten:

> Fortunately the gun is pointed down at the pavement for suddenly – BANG! – and you feel a thump on the calf of your left leg. A torrent of expletives from [Maj] Hank [Caldwell, Royal Regiment of Canada] tells that his knees have taken the brunt of concrete bits dislodged by the bullet ricocheting off the sidewalk. He pulls up his pant-legs and starts picking cinder-like bits out of his kneecaps. Your leg is wet ... you pull up your pant-leg and see two little holes where the bullet passed in and out.

> 'That's the third time this morning it's done that,' says the soldier in wonderment, pulling back the cocking-lever of the Sten now pointing directly at your stomach. Pushing the muzzle away from you, you tell him, 'For God's sake, man, put it on safety!' In obvious bewilderment he asks, 'What's that?'
>
> Hearing this, Hank demands, 'Where the hell did you get your weapons training, soldier?' Says the soldier apologetically, 'I never had any weapons training, sir. I was as cook until I was sent up to the Royals.' (Tout 2003: 68)

On 24 October 1944 Cpl Cliff Brown of The Lincoln and Welland Regiment, a Canadian Infantry unit, found that his Sten failed him during the fighting on the Belgian–Dutch border: 'We had to clear the barn as we knew there were Germans inside firing at our advance. My men flung the door open and I attempted to spray the interior with my Sten gun. It failed to fire. However the Germans in the barn immediately gave up. The Sten gun was an unpredictable weapon. Not my first such experience. But it was a very effective weapon 99% of the time' (Tout 2003: 169).

A Sten was issued to each Commonwealth tank crew along with their vehicle, for close-range defence and foot patrolling. Some desert veterans resented having to give up their Shermans (issued with Thompsons) in exchange for Cromwells (issued with Stens); a few disregarded regulations and retained their Thompsons. Sgt Jake Wardrop, an M4A4 Sherman VC 'Firefly' tank commander of 5th Royal Tank Regiment, was tragically killed in April 1945, but left a colourful diary of his wartime experiences. Wardrop had used a 'tommy gun' in the desert, but records several instances where the newly issued Stens came in handy, as in this episode while patrolling west of Nistelrode in The Netherlands in September 1944:

> One day we had some fun and Lt [Keith] Crocker [Wardrop's troop leader] showed what a stout little man he was. We were pushing along a track where nobody had been before and as always Lt Crocker was leading followed by [Sgt] Snowy [Harris, another tank commander in C Squadron] then me. We reached a crossroad and I saw Lt Crocker

A soldier of 15th (Scottish) Division armed with a Mk III takes cover beneath a jeep during Operation *Epsom*, Normandy, 26 June 1944. This photograph illustrates the advantage of the Sten's side-loading magazine as it allows the soldier to assume a much lower shooting position than with a bottom-loading magazine. Because so much of the fighting in the *bocage* during the break-out from the Normandy beachhead was at close quarters, the Sten proved a very effective weapon for meeting engagements against German soldiers. (IWM B 5998)

nip down from his tank firing his revolver into the ditch, Snowy jumped down also with his sten gun so I cocked the .5[in Browning M2 turret-mounted machine gun] and put a burst into the trees ahead. There were ten Boches [Germans] in the ditch with rifles, Spandaus and some of the new 'tank-terror' rockets [Panzerfausts]. Lt Crocker had seen them and as his [7.92mm Besa] machine gun could not depress far enough to get on to them he had attacked them with his revolver on foot and a very stout show it was. They surrendered of course except for two who ran for it and escaped. (Forty 2009: 196)

IRREGULAR SUBMACHINE GUNS: THE STEN WITH SOE, OSS, AND THE RESISTANCE

Britain's highly secret Special Operations Executive (SOE) was formed on 22 July 1940 to conduct guerrilla warfare against Nazi Germany and its allies, and to train and assist resistance movements in countries occupied by the Axis Powers. The US Office of Strategic Services (OSS), forerunner of the Central Intelligence Agency, was established on 13 June 1942 to assemble and assess strategic information for the Joint Chiefs of Staff, and to carry out special operations, including propaganda, espionage and subversion activities. Both these organizations sought to foment, train and supply resistance movements in those countries overrun by the Axis Powers.

Col (later Maj-Gen Sir) Colin Gubbins, responsible for the formation of Britain's Auxiliary Units, was the driving force behind SOE. He realized that the submachine gun, ideally one that could utilize captured ammunition, was an ideal guerrilla weapon – easy to use, easy to conceal, light, and devastating at close ranges (Foot 1999: 10). Accordingly, the Sten quickly became the preferred arm of many of the US and British special-forces personnel who worked with Resistance movements. In his master's thesis on Col Aaron Bank and the early of days of US Special Forces, Darren Sapp makes a good comparison of the Sten and the AK-47 for guerrilla usage:

Most Jedburghs achieved firearms competency, but the role as a teacher and operator meant they needed a wide proficiency with weapons used by various nations and the ability to build and implement explosives. Basic point and shoot firing is one skill, but the adaptability to use a captured weapon requires immense training due to multifarious clip feeds, ammunition, safeties, inherent problems, effectiveness, etc. The reason the AK-47 has been in wide use in the last forty years – particularly for soldiers of limited training, such as guerillas – is its simple application. It is easy to learn to use and clean, and rarely it fails. During World War II, the Sten gun served this purpose and became the main weapon for resistance forces. It was a handheld submachine gun weighing about eight pounds loaded. Jedburghs received much training on the Sten, and it is the weapon most commonly mentioned in their memoirs.

A member of the Danish Resistance unpacks a drop container holding Mk II Stens, ammunition, grenades and other items. (Danish Resistance Museum)

Jedburgh teams, which took their name from the town of Jedburgh in Scotland, consisted of three men, including a radio operator, and normally included British or American personnel plus at least one member from the country in which the team was to operate. The Jedburghs parachuted in, then worked closely with Resistance groups, giving them a link to Allied headquarters and also supplying expertise in weapons, explosives, tactics, etc. The Jedburgh teams in France were keenly aware of the risks their activities posed to members of the local population, and so had to be scrupulously careful about removing all traces of their activities, as Sgt Gordon Tack of Jedburgh Team 'Giles' recalled:

> The Germans knew that we stayed in farmhouses. We answered that by getting up at dawn and did a forced march eight or ten miles away in rough, wooded country, and stayed there until late in the day when we moved to another farm ... But if they found any evidence of our occupation, they killed the farmers. They normally shut them up in the farmhouse and set fire to the farmhouse or just shot them. In one instance they found one Sten round, just an ordinary 9-millimetre Sten round, amongst the straw of the haystack where we'd slept, and on the strength of that they killed a whole family and burned the farm down. (Bailey 2008b: 227)

SOE operatives were active in many parts of occupied Europe, including regions such as Albania, where resistance was already overt and widespread. In such areas SOE operatives wore uniform, unlike their colleagues in North-West Europe. Having been trained to use a wide variety of weapons, both Allied and Axis, operatives didn't necessarily opt for the Sten, however:

> With personal arms, some choice was allowed. Often men were led to the armoury and told to pick what they wanted. 'It was like Christmas Day,' one officer recalled. 'We were shown this storeroom which had every sort of armament you could think of: German pistols, Japanese fighting knives, every sort of weapon. And I thought, "I'll have one of those, one of those, one of those".' In the end he took a [.45 ACP] Marlin-Hyde M2 [submachine gun], an American weapon of very limited make; others chose Schmeissers (MP 40s], Thompsons and [9mm] Welguns, the latter an SOE-developed sub-machine gun [that used Sten magazines mounted vertically]. 'After careful consideration I chose a Smith & Wesson revolver and a dagger,' [Sgt] Bob Melrose remembered. 'I was given a box of 50 rounds of .38 ammo for the revolver with the instruction that this would be all I would get and advised to obtain an enemy weapon and ammo locally.' (Bailey 2008a: 52–53)

Some Resistance fighters grew very fond of their Stens. Col Graeme Warrack, 1st Airborne Division's senior medical officer, was captured at Arnhem but escaped in October 1944 and sheltered with the Dutch Resistance until February 1945. He later recalled his experiences during The Netherlands' grim 'Hunger Winter':

> We trudged through the snow to Joop's house, where we found Dick cleaning his Webley .45. Two other men were there: Jan, who had a handshake like a vice, and 'Sten Gun Lou', a magnificent character who never parted from his Sten and was quite prepared to use it. These two were to be our new guides.
>
> After a time, Lou came in and announced that thirty-five Germans were spending the night at the next farm, about 30 yards away. Dick patted his pistol and Sten Gun Lou grinned at his weapon. Luckily it was 10:00 p.m. by then, so the Germans would be unlikely to disturb us. We hoped for the best—our best, not Sten Gun Lou's best. (Warrack 1968: 206)

This photograph of Dule Bey Allemani, an Albanian tribal chief, holding a Mk II was taken by SOE operative Maj David Smiley at Lure in July 1944, during the second SOE mission to Albania. (IWM HU 64787)

The Sten was a highly effective ambush weapon – when it worked. Jozef Gabcík and Jan Kubiš, along with seven other Czech soldiers in exile, were airlifted into occupied Czechoslovakia in December 1941; their mission was to assassinate SS-Obergruppenführer Reinhard Heydrich, the acting Reichsprotektor of Bohemia and Moravia and a key architect of the Nazis' 'Final Solution'. The operation, codenamed *Anthropoid*, took place on 27 May 1942, along the route of Heydrich's daily car journey from his home to Prague Castle. Lt Col Peter Wilkinson, a staff officer in the Czech–Polish Section at SOE headquarters, recalled the mission, in which a Sten – a Mk II – played a key role:

> I think the original plan was that they should be armed with Colt Super .38 pistols and they were certainly trained to be Deadeye Dicks with them. We had always taken the view that a sub-machine gun was really far too bulky to carry on an operation of this sort. However, for some reason or other, a Sten gun was included in their load list, probably at the personal request of one or two of the chaps. I would certainly not myself consciously have sanctioned it if I'd personally approved the load list, which I don't think I did.
>
> The plan, as far as we knew it, was that in some way Heydrich's car was to be held up and at that moment one or both of them should

throw one of these special bombs against the side of the car. The bombs had been designed to cause the bodywork of the car to fragment and not to fragment themselves, like a Mills bomb: they were an adaptation of a bomb used in the Western Desert to attack tanks. And of course it was extremely successful. Although the Sten gun [fired by Gabcík] jammed, the car did slow down and the second chap [Kubiš] did throw a bomb, which exploded against the side of the car, and, as a result, a piece of poisoned clothing or something got into Heydrich's wound, from which he died [on 4 June]. (Bailey 2008b: 114–16)

Gabcík and Kubiš fled the scene, convinced their attempt had failed; they were hunted down and killed by German forces on 18 June. In reprisal, the Germans murdered all 173 men of the village of Lidice (spuriously associated with those who participated in Operation *Anthropoid*) burned the village to the ground and deported its women and children to concentration camps.

The simplicity of the Sten's operation was a key factor in its suitability for the guerrilla fighters of the Resistance, many of whom, it was assumed, would require extensive training. In occupied France during 1944, however, SOE arms and sabotage instructor Capt Peter Lake found that many of the Resistance fighters he was instructing were already well versed in guerrilla warfare:

In fact most of them were refugees from Spain and particularly from Catalonia. I spent several days in the Maquis and instead of being able to give them tuition in the use of plastic explosive and the use of the Sten gun, in French, I found that I had to do it largely in Spanish, assisted by a few words of Catalan. A lot of them had already been extensively trained in subversive methods and moving around the countryside without being seen ... They weren't afraid of anything or anybody. (Bailey 2008b: 208)

Many European Resistance groups manufactured their own Stens. Despite the fact that the Sten was designed to be easily produced, even in small shops, the UK Ministry of Supply refused to drop plans to build the Sten to Resistance groups. That doesn't mean that skilled mechanics didn't disassemble Stens dropped to Resistance groups and attempt to produce – and in some cases succeed in producing – Sten copies locally. However, these copies generally did not conform exactly to the original.

Among the best-known of these Resistance Stens are those produced by the Danish Resistance. In August 1942, the first Stens were dropped to Danish Resistance fighters. Included in the drop containers with the Stens were instructions in Danish for their use. Up to May 1945, approximately 3,000 Stens were air-dropped to the Danes, while a further 1,000 or so were delivered by sea from Sweden. It is important to note that the Sten was certainly not the only submachine gun available to Danish Resistance fighters. Danish Resistance Museum photograph archives contain many photographs of Danish fighters armed with variations of the Suomi, rather than with the Sten.

Four Danish Resistance groups produced versions of the Sten locally. Since drawings were usually created from Stens that had been air-dropped, they did not always match dimensions of British-produced Stens completely, though some were close enough that parts were interchangeable. Barrels for Danish Resistance Stens were often stolen from the Suomi production line at Dansk Rekylriffel Syndikat (Danish Recoil Rifle Syndicate) in Copenhagen, or produced from worn-out rifle barrels. At least some of the Danish Stens had the magazine well altered to take Suomi magazines, which could also be stolen and supplied to the Resistance.

Stens were produced in bicycle shops, machine shops at shipyards or other maintenance facilities, and hidden amid other work. In addition to the use of Suomi magazines, other variations found on some Stens include: a pistol grip instead of the 'skeleton' stock, so that the weapon could be concealed more readily; lack of sights; and (among those produced at the shipyard) use of aluminium alloy for parts such as the magazine housing, stock, trigger and trigger-mechanism cover. It is estimated that approximately 1,000 Stens were produced by the various Danish Resistance groups. For anyone interested in the Danish Resistance Sten, the author recommends visiting the Danish Resistance Museum in Copenhagen, which features a reconstruction of a bicycle shop of the sort used to produce Stens.

Stens were also produced in Norway for the MILORG, the primary Resistance group. As with the Danish Resistance, acquiring barrels appeared to be the major roadblock to building Stens, but thanks to one Norwegian who had observed Kentucky rifles being built in the United States prior to World War II, a simple machine was constructed to rifle Sten barrels. Drawings for Sten parts were made in such a way that they were not recognizable as such, and many small parts were made at various workshops where they were unrecognizable as gun parts. Even the people involved in these Stens' manufacture did not always know what they were making; workers producing barrels were convinced they were making drive shafts, having been shown carefully prepared false drawings of the 'drive shaft'. For those that were obviously gun parts, workers known to be loyal to the Resistance were chosen.

Once the parts were gathered, they were assembled in a basement workshop and tested using a car muffler as a 'silencer'. The assembly point was later moved to a secret room in an Oslo machine works. Magazines were made in another local factory at night since they would be recognizable if seen by other workers or during German inspections. Locals who saw the shop operating at night assumed it was working overtime for Germans and speculated that it might be attacked by the Resistance! Production of Norwegian Stens continued until May 1945, with around 800 eventually being manufactured.

The Sten was enough of an icon for the Danish Resistance that they circulated this cartoon about it. (Danish Resistance Museum)

Danish Resistance fighters in May 1945; the one at right is armed with a Mk II. The armbands identify Resistance members. (Danish Resistance Museum)

Polish Resistance groups were involved in the manufacture of a wide variety of Stens, some virtually handmade by local blacksmiths while others were produced in machine shops by skilled craftsmen. Quality varied widely as did many design features. One version, for example, was designed with only the pistol grip, to allow concealment. A Warsaw metalworking shop produced thousands of barrels for clandestine Stens and Radom pistols. Around 1,300 Polish Resistance Stens of all types were reportedly produced.

The Warsaw Uprising of August–October 1944, in which it is estimated that 16,000 Resistance fighters were killed and another 6,000 wounded, saw use of the Sten. Few Polish Resistance Stens have survived, at least in some part due to the heavy casualties suffered by the Polish Home Army and other Resistance fighters during the Uprising (Laidler 2000: 201). Because the Sten could easily be concealed, it could be readily transported by Resistance fighters. Since they did not have a ready supply of ammunition, its ability to use captured German 9mm ammunition was invaluable. Since many weapons available to the Resistance were older sporting arms or rifles, the firepower of the Sten was also very useful in the close-quarters fighting during the Uprising. Both airdropped Stens and locally produced ones were among the most effective weapons available to the desperate Poles.

Bicycle-shop armourers **(previous pages)**

As Danish Resistance operatives pick up newly assembled Stens from a bicycle-repair shop mechanic south of Copenhagen in 1944, two men of the Schalberg Korpset, the Danish SS organization, arrive on the scene.

Many barrels used to build Danish Stens were made from Suomi submachine-gun parts smuggled out of the factory by Resistance sympathisers. Also on the workbench is a Danish M1891 Ordnance Revolver.

THE STEN IN THE FAR EAST

With the Japanese entry into the war, British and Commonwealth forces became engaged in defence of British possessions in the Far East. Fighting the Japanese brought new challenges, for which new weapons were required. Commonwealth forces soon found themselves involved in jungle warfare, which meant close-combat weapons such as submachine guns were at a premium. The August 1942 training manual *Forest, Bush and Jungle Warfare Against a Modern Enemy* stressed the importance of appropriately armed infantry:

> Infantry will remain the general purpose arm ... Fighting in close country makes it desirable that infantry should be specially equipped for this purpose. Some form of hatchet (dah, machet or kukri) is essential ... Machine carbines [SMGs], pistols, light rifles, and knives are useful alternatives to service rifles and bayonets, which are apt to encumber men in thick forests. Because of the frequent possibility of being surprised, ability to fire weapons quickly and accurately at short ranges, as well as training to fire suddenly from the hip, is very necessary. (Quoted in Bull 2007: 23)

The crew of a jeep stand ready with Stens beside their vehicle during an encounter with the Japanese in the advance on Mandalay, February 1945. (IWM SE 3111)

Accordingly, the Thompson was widely issued to Commonwealth troops in the Far East and proved to be a popular and useful jungle-fighting weapon. In 1944 and 1945, though, the smaller and lighter Sten came to be used in increasing numbers, although the Australians preferred the Owen and some British units acquired the US .30 M1 Carbine for officers and NCOs, owing to its handiness and longer range (Brayley 2002b: 39).

As with their counterparts in other theatres, a ten-man infantry section in the Far East carried a variety of weapons: the section leader, normally a corporal, was armed with a Sten, while a lance-corporal or experienced private carried the section's .303in Bren light machine gun; the other eight men were armed with .303in Lee-Enfield bolt-action rifles. The section's basic complement of ammunition was made up of 160× 9mm rounds for the Sten in five magazines (assuming 32 rounds per magazine), 800 rounds of .303in ammunition in five-round chargers (for rifle use), 21× 30-round Bren magazines, and ten grenades; of course, additional ammunition was also carried as needed (Brayley 2002b: 37–40).

Between 4 April and 22 June 1944, British and Indian forces decisively checked the Japanese invasion of India. The prolonged fighting involved the recapture of positions on Kohima Ridge from the Japanese, and during that May 2nd Battalion, The Royal Norfolk Regiment, played a key role in the battle. Capt Dickie Davies' Sten let him down in the brutal close-quarter struggle for the bunkers: 'Four Japanese ran out of one of the bunkers. I pressed the trigger, and nothing bloody well happened – my Sten gun jammed. They always jammed, a useless weapon. I threw it at them I was so annoyed' (Thompson 2010: 238). CSM Walter Gidding of Davies' battalion led from the front: 'I had a Sten gun and I was firing, scrambling up, grabbing hold of a tree, firing the Sten, going a little further, encouraging the lads. You couldn't see the bunkers or slits, they were so well camouflaged' (Thompson 2010: 243).

FIRING THE STEN

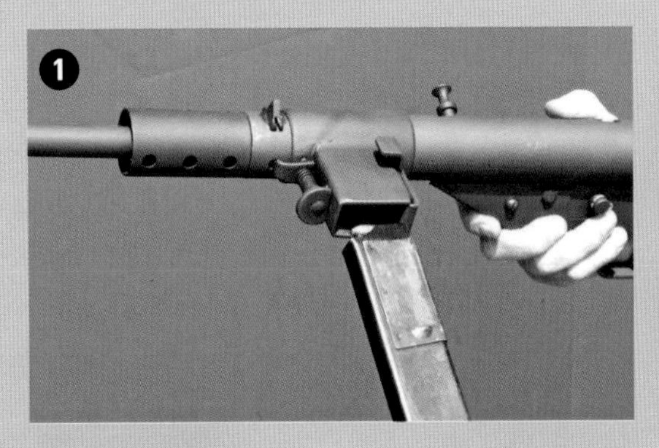

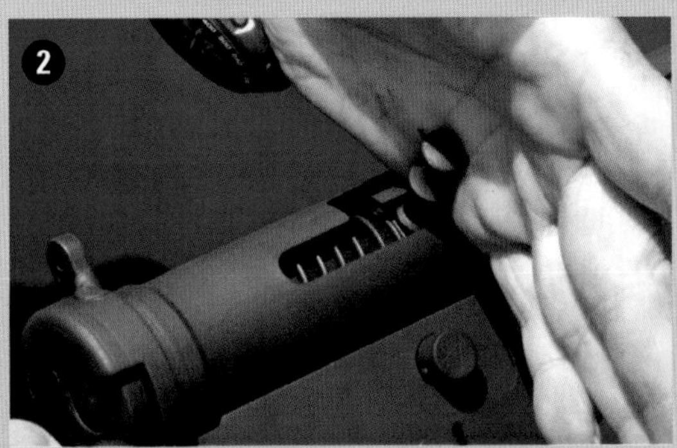

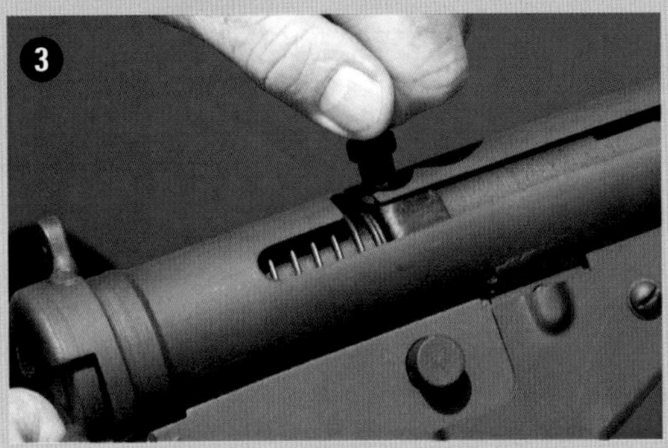

When a loaded magazine was inserted into the magazine well, it was important to make sure it was thrust all the way in until it locked **(1)**. Normally, a smack with the palm of the hand ensured the magazine was fully seated. It was very important to bear in mind when inserting a magazine with the bolt open that the weapon was ready to fire at that point and a pull on the trigger or a jar to the gun could cause it to begin firing on full-automatic. Many injuries were caused to troops using the Sten due to such accidental and negligent discharges. With the magazine in place, if the bolt was closed it was pulled to the rear to cock the Sten **(2)**. Drill taught with the Mk II (illustrated here) was to reach over with the left hand to cock the weapon. Note that when cocking the Sten with a loaded magazine in place a round is ready to fire; therefore, if the cocking handle slipped from the hand the weapon could fire. To put the Sten on Safe the bolt handle was rotated into the slot cut into the Sten's receiver **(3)**.

AFTER WORLD WAR II

From 1948 onwards, Commonwealth forces saw extensive service in the 12-year Malayan Emergency, and Stens were widely issued. Settlers and Malayan police were also armed with Stens, though a British Pathé newsreel from December 1952 shows settlers trading in their Stens for US M1 Carbines and also shows members of the Malay police training with the M1 Carbine.

The Korean War of 1950–53 meant that a large contingent of British service personnel, many of whom were National Servicemen, were deployed to the Far East. World War II-era small arms were still standard issue; for example, Pte Dave Green of 1st Battalion, the Gloucestershire Regiment, carried a Lee-Enfield in Korea before his capture at the battle of the Imjin River in April 1951. Green recalled his involvement in operations against North Korean guerrillas, in which the Sten once again proved its value in

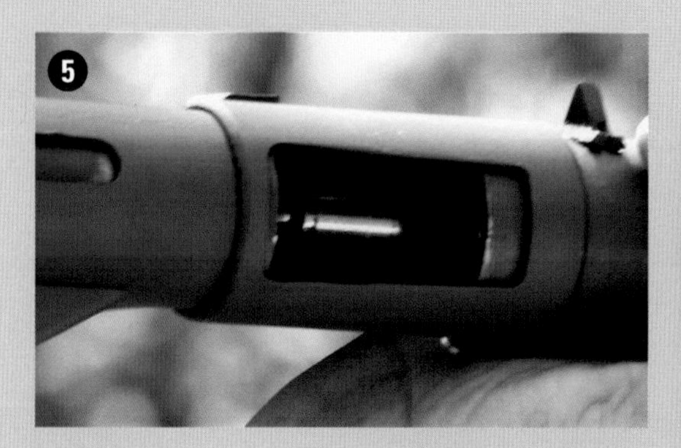

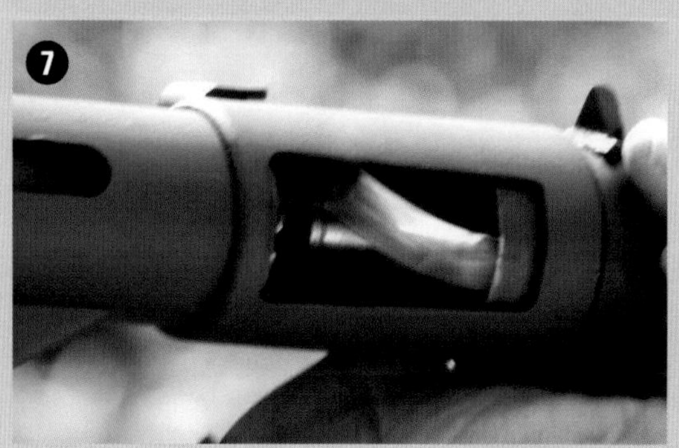

Though better than no safety at all, this was still an unreliable method of rendering the weapon safe as the bolt handle could jar out of the slot if the weapon were dropped or it struck a hard surface. For full-automatic fire the crossbolt selector had to be pushed through so that it protruded to the left. When it protruded to the right, as shown here **(4)**, the weapon was set for semi-automatic fire. To fire the Sten it was raised to the shoulder and the stock pressed against the shoulder. Note that when the Sten is cocked the loaded magazine is visible through the ejection port **(5)**. The Sten was relatively controllable if fired in short bursts **(6)**; however, the author has found that the 'skeleton' stock tends to slide down on the shoulder as the muzzle rises in recoil. Recoil is moderate and little movement right or left is noticed. Once an empty case is ejected **(7)**, the bolt runs forward to chamber and fire the next round. To remove a magazine it is grasped as the release lever is depressed with the thumb **(8)**.

close-range ambush situations: 'As [Sgt] Jock [McKay] and I reached the top, we came across a bedraggled group of about thirty guerillas, sitting around their fire. Jock at once opened fire with his Sten gun whilst I engaged a man standing not twenty yards away, firing my rifle from the hip. He just stared at me as he dropped, his hands still in his coat pockets' (Green 2003: 42).

Canadian forces deployed to Korea with 1st Commonwealth Division were also still equipped with the Sten, but reinforcements were found to have had deficient weapons training:

> Early in May 1953 the Director General of Military Training, Brigadier G. Walsh, asked Brigadier Allard for detailed reports on the condition of future drafts. Such a report, submitted to Allard in mid-June by the commander of the Canadian Detachment of the Divisional Battle School, clearly confirmed what had previously been reflected only in general remarks: the proficiency of reinforcements reaching the theatre was far below standard. Citing individual cases in detail, the report stated that the majority of reinforcements required basic instruction on all weapons – very few had received any on the Sten – and their small knowledge of fieldcraft was mainly theoretical. At the same time, most were quite receptive to training and anxious to join their units in the field. (Wood 1966: 281)

In postwar Cyprus, from where British forces sought to protect the Suez Canal, tensions between the Greek and Turkish communities and the former's desire for union with Greece escalated into an 'Emergency' in 1955 as a bloody terrorist campaign began. British forces were pitched into combat with EOKA guerrillas equipped with captured British arms, pitting Sten against Sten.

Capt Sandy Cavenagh, a medical officer in 3rd Parachute Battalion, was serving in Cyprus during 1956 on counterinsurgency operations. As a medical officer, Cavenagh treated men injured by accidental or negligent discharges of the Sten. He cites various instances such as this one:

> Whenever you went out of camp you carried a loaded weapon and each vehicle carried an escort facing backwards. Weapons were loaded as soon as you left camp. Rifles and Bren guns were comparatively safe, as it was difficult to forget where they were pointing, and the triggers needed firm pressure to set them off. The 9mm pistol and particularly the Sten gun were the culprits. Both were short and swung easily in any direction. The Sten gun could be set off by a good blow on the butt or by being dropped. The worst accidents had occurred when escorts had accidentally dropped or knocked Sten guns, sending off fire through their drivers. Yet considering battalion had only handled live ammunition on the range before coming to Cyprus the number of accidents was not excessive. (Cavenagh 1965: 59)

The instances mentioned by Cavenagh above can mostly be attributed to negligence, but when he discussed problems with the Sten during 3rd

Men of A Company, 3rd Parachute Battalion, after taking the buildings at El Gamil airfield during Operation *Musketeer*, the Anglo-French invasion of Egypt, in November 1956. Note the soldier with a Mk V at the left. (IWM HU 4196)

Parachute Battalion's Suez jump, it seems the gun itself was at fault. The Suez Crisis of 1956 was the last time British parachute forces jumped into battle. Cavenagh was particularly scathing about the Sten:

> At least Lamph had time in which to get his rifle out. His companions who landed at the edge of the airfield were under fire at once at close range. It took them thirty long seconds to get their weapons ready to shoot back. What they said later about the Sims weapons container cannot be printed. The Sten gun was described in similar language. It had been widely and successfully used in Europe during the war, but in sand it very quickly seized up. It was galling that many other units, even some policemen in Cyprus, were issued with the much more efficient Lanchester submachine-gun. In Egypt the parachutists cursed their stopped guns, threw them away and replaced them with the much better Berettas, Schmeissers or Russian carbines with which their enemies were armed. Everyone felt that a little more government expenditure on transport aircraft and good infantry weapons would have made their jobs a lot easier. (Cavenagh 1965: 129–30)

Cavenagh also comments that the British paras felt their Stens were greatly inferior, in terms of reliability and stopping power, to the MAS 36 CR 49 rifles, MAT 49 submachine guns and US M1 and M2 carbines[5] used by the French airborne troops who also jumped at Suez; the French fired their weapons immediately on landing, while the British had to retrieve theirs from leg bags or containers (Turner 2006: 361). Cavenagh offers other instances of Sten guns malfunctioning during the operation.

By the time of Suez the British Commandos had also adopted the Sten in place of their cherished Thompsons. Marine A.R. Ashton of No. 45 Commando recalled the preparations for the Suez landings:

[5] I am grateful to Martin Windrow for this information

> Even as I took a closer look at 45 Commando, it was beginning to take on an increasingly aggressive and combative experience ... Sten gun magazines were taped end to end to enable a quick change under pressure. Mysteriously – for they were not official issue – blue steel Commando knives appeared from nowhere; their unmistakeable hilts protruding menacingly from magazine holders and other makeshift scabbards. Our boot-blacked webbing was camouflaged with strips of Hessian and scrim; brasses and cap badges were dulled; desert-warfare goggles issued; grenades primed with short fuses; ammo compressed carefully into Bren and Sten magazines ... One could not escape the fact that this was for real. This was no exercise. (Turner 2006: 336)

Once the British and French forces were established on land, they sometimes found Stens in the hands of their enemies, as Capt Roger T. Booth of 3rd Parachute Battalion related:

> Lurking at the junction to our left was a large excited crowd in ambush. I saw the French jeep [that had been attacked in the incident Booth had been ordered to investigate] slewed on the pavement, its bonnet roasted black and pink in an attempt to set fire to it. There were men and women, children and youths swaying en masse with excitement.
>
> There in their forefront most vivid of all was a tall erect old man with a short grey beard, turbaned and wearing a greenish gelabehah. At his shoulder, clamped in aim at us, was a sten gun. I remember thinking 'Thank god it's a sten', a weapon not blessed with great accuracy over but a short distance. I could see other weapons brandished in the crowd. It was cabaret time...
>
> The boulevard seemed infinitely grand in its width. The juddering burst from the sten gun sprayed past us. Our driver, an intelligent soldier, had rammed his boot on the accelerator at the sound of the first shot. His instinct was now paying off... We roared away unscathed while heavy firing still thundered behind us. (Turner 2006: 418–19)

A decade later, US units of MACV SOG (Military Assistance Command Vietnam, Special Operations Group) were still using suppressed Stens for clandestine operations in Vietnam. Reconnaissance operators often chose the Mk II (S) for snatches of enemy prisoners:

Suppressed Stens in Vietnam **(opposite)**

In mid-1967 on the Laos/Vietnam border, a six-man MACV-SOG reconnaissance team (RT) hidden in heavy jungle are ambushing a Viet Cong tax collector and his two bodyguards along a jungle trail, in order to snatch the tax collector for interrogation. The two US SOG operators are armed with the Stens and have shot the tax collector's two guards – one behind him and another in front – without hitting him. Indigenous members of the RT, in this case Montagnards, crouch ready to grab the tax collector to take him for interrogation. The positions of the RT's members is important so only the two guards get shot and only the two with suppressed Stens shoot.

The preferred submachine gun for prisoner snatches was the British Sten Mk IIS because it could be disassembled quickly and stored compactly in a rucksack. This enabled a recon man to carry a more powerful AK or CAR-15 and employ the low-powered suppressed weapon only during a prisoner snatch. A World War II development for the British Special Operations Executive (SOE) – which ran secret agents and saboteurs in Occupied Europe – the suppressed Sten was best suited for close-range shooting. In semiauto mode it was reasonably accurate and fairly quiet, although the recoiling bolt's 'clack-clack-clack' seemed unnecessarily noisy. (Plaster 2000: 142)

STENS IN OTHER HANDS

Along with a huge array of other World War II-era weapons, Stens were widely used by all sides in the escalating violence in the British Mandate for Palestine in the 1940s, as vicious guerrilla warfare between the Arab and Jewish communities gave way to a conventional inter-state war between the emergent State of Israel and the invading Arab armies. Noted military historian Uri Milstein, whose father served in the British Army as a volunteer in World War II and is himself a veteran of the Six-Day War of 1967 and the Yom Kippur War of 1973, notes an incident before Independence that demonstrates the role Sten guns played in the fighting. When the Palestine Police Force, an armed British organization responsible for maintaining law and order in Mandatory Palestine, refused to confront an Arab mob, Michel Rotem, who instructed GADNA (a paramilitary youth training organization) youth corps cadets at the Hebrew High School, decided it was time to take action:

Students had formed a line in the street; Yisra'el Punt and a weapons officer named Kretchmer were issuing orders. Punt told me to help. 'We're taking emergency action,' he said. They got out a sack of hand-to-hand combat weapons and passed them around. Kretchmer brought out a leather bag with a Sten gun.

'Who knows how to use a Sten?' we were asked.

'I'm familiar with the gun,' I answered.

'Right,' said Kretchmer. 'He was in the Brigade' [formed from volunteers from Palestine, the British Army's Jewish Brigade served in Italy and then Northern Europe during World War II].

I assembled the Sten and tied a clip on [possibly to retain the magazine while making the weapon easier to conceal]. They told me not to snap the clip in so it wouldn't attract attention. I hid the Sten under my

Surplus World War II British weapons were in common use during the Israeli war of independence. Here, in 1948 Jewish truck guards are pictured armed with Stens. (Cody Images)

sweater and we headed for Mamilla. I was second in line. Punt said, 'You from the Brigade, let me go first.'

We climbed into a truck waiting for us along the way and filled it with stones. I was the only one with a gun. We drove to The [Assicurazioni] Generali [insurance company] building. The road was blocked by British armored cars. We got off the truck.

Punt dickered with a Jewish police officer, Sofer, and a British one named Tiger. Punt adopted such an authoritative tone that Tiger agreed to let small groups filter into Mamilla.

A British policeman spotted my Sten when I passed the roadblock, but Tiger motioned him to let me go. There was a feeling that we were acting on behalf of the British.

Stores were burning in the commercial center. Orders came to enter any building still not in flames, assemble the Jews and help them get away. We collected them by the Triangle Building and escorted them to the Russian Compound. (Milstein 1997)

During Operation *Scaramouche* in 1954, members of a British Army patrol search a captured Mau Mau suspect near Kanyuki, Kenya. Note the Sten carried by the soldier at the left. (Cody Images)

Rotem recalled that another Sten was issued to a former member of the Jewish Brigade to help rescue students from the university complex on Mount Scopus.

At least some Stens were manufactured by the Hagana, the underground military organization, prior to Israel's 1948 War of Independence. But it seems likely that far more were obtained from British military stores than were actually made in clandestine workshops. Many of those made in such workshops had unrifled barrels, making them inaccurate at distances further than a few yards (Laidler 2000: 218).

The Sten also saw extensive use in Kenya on both sides during the Mau Mau Rebellion, an anti-colonial uprising between 1952 and 1960. Some settlers had been issued Sten guns for self-defence. Mau Mau guerrillas also used captured Sten guns. In *Mau Mau Memoirs*, Marshall S. Clough describes the arms of a Mau Mau band:

Though the movement did obtain some weapons in Nairobi before the Emergency, there were nowhere enough to go around; when General Matenjagwo [a Mau Mau leader later killed by soldiers of The King's African Rifles, including Idi Amin] entered the forest with 250 men, his force had 6 sten guns, 20 rifles, and 6 pistols. Large guerrilla bands like the group assembled at Kariaini Headquarters camp in mid-1953 had a wider assortment of European weapons, including occasionally bren guns, usually sten guns, .303 rifles, .44 rifles, shotguns, and various caliber pistols, but most of the men were armed with *simis*, *pangas* [heavy hacking knives of the machete type], and homemade guns. (Clough 1997: 148)

Carrying the Sten safely

Because of the danger of negligent and accidental discharges with the Sten, experienced users developed the technique of using their hand as a 'safety'. Here, the bolt is forward on an empty chamber and a loaded magazine is in place. By carrying the Sten with the edge of the hand against the cocking handle, even if the Sten is jarred the bolt cannot come back and fire.

There was a second method for using the hand when the Sten's bolt is cocked and a loaded magazine is in place. By carrying the Sten with the hand in front of the bolt, it could not be jarred to go off. Note that neither of these techniques for carrying the Sten with the hand blocking the bolt would have served in a patrolling situation in which an enemy might be encountered at any time; instead, the Sten would have been carried in the 'ready' position. However, when getting into and out of vehicles or otherwise moving with the Sten, using the hand to block the bolt handle was a good technique.

The Thompson submachine gun – the Tommy Gun – has been an iconic arm with the Irish Republican Army to the extent that it has been celebrated in more than one IRA song. However, the IRA also used the Sten. The Sten was an excellent weapon choice for the IRA as it would fit beneath a trench coat and 9mm ammunition was relatively easy to acquire. It would appear, too, from some captured examples that if a Sten were damaged, parts could be salvaged and another weapon cobbled together in a local shop. In *The Sten Machine Carbine*, for example, Peter Laidler illustrates two Stens captured from the IRA by British Security Forces. Both used an assortment of parts from British Stens. One was 'sterile' with no serial number and may have been an SOE gun, while the other combined a Mk II front end and Mk III rear end welded to a receiver made from a length of tubing.

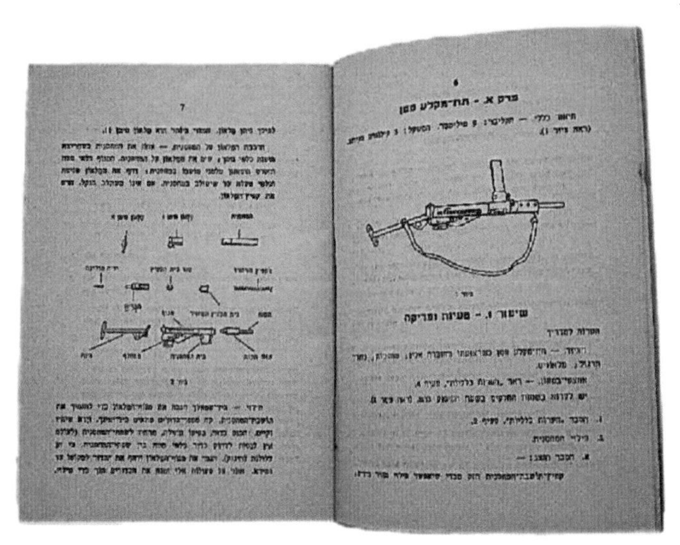

פרק א. - תת-מקלע סטן

The interior of an Israeli manual for the Sten, which was widely used during the 1948 War of Independence. (Author)

Just as Stens had been constructed in Resistance workshops on the continent of Europe, it appears that at least a few were assembled in Ireland. The Royal Ulster Constabulary used Sten guns and at least a few may have fallen into IRA hands at one time or another. Of course, the British Army was probably the largest source of Stens for the IRA. In Bernard O'Riain's *Running to Stand Still*, he states:

A Sten formerly used by the IRA; note the addition of the front pistol grip. Although the IRA often cobbled together Stens with parts from various guns, this one appears to be based on a Mk II. (Copyright Collector Grade Publications, Inc.)

> The Sunday papers in June 1954 carry the biggest headlines I've ever seen. A Bedford truck pulled up outside Gough Barracks [Armagh City], the largest British Army barracks in Northern Ireland. Two men walked up to the British Army guard, put a gun in his ribs, and invited him to walk with them to the guardhouse. There the rest of the soldiers on duty were informed that they were now prisoners of the Irish Republican Army. Would they please lie down and allow themselves to be tied up? This they did, whether out of astonishment or the heat of the day, we don't know. The IRA was supposed to have died in the late forties, and these soldiers have never heard of it. Neither has the rest of Ireland.
>
> The lads loaded the lorry with Lee-Enfield rifles, Bren guns, Sten guns, and thousands of rounds of ammunition. 'The armoury was emptied,' cry the papers. (O'Riain 2005: 132)

The Gough Barracks was chosen as a target at least partially because an IRA man noticed that the sentry on duty outside the barracks did not have a magazine in his Sten. After this, according to O'Riain, a young IRA member joined the British Army and was posted to the Gough Barracks to gather inside intelligence. The IRA team that raided the armoury was armed with Thompson submachine guns among other arms, but they left with plenty of other automatic weapons including 50 Sten guns and 12 Bren guns. After locking the British soldiers in the guardroom, the IRA men took every key they could find and locked every door they encountered from the outside. As a final indignity to the British Army, those keys were later auctioned in the United States to raise money for the IRA! During the 1950s other armoury raids garnered more Sten guns for the IRA.

Penalties for possession of a Sten could be harsh for members of the IRA. Padraigh McKearney, for example, was sentenced in 1980 to 14 years for possession of a loaded Sten gun. However, he escaped Maze Prison on 25 September 1983 and was never recaptured.

In the 1950s Stens even found their way to Cuba, where revolutionary forces under Fidel Castro toppled the Batista regime. The American William Alexander Morgan, who fought with the revolutionary forces, explained why he favoured the Sten (and Sterling) over the Thompson and M3 'grease gun' – it was down to the British weapons' lighter weight and recoil and greater effective range. 'Furthermore ... weight difference between 9 mm ammo and .45 makes a hell of a difference in favor of the 9 mm when you're off on a 40 mile hike in the Cuban backwoods' (Brown 1959: 17).

IMPACT

Imitation and influence

A September 1943 article in the US magazine *Popular Science* offered an interesting example of the Sten as a propaganda symbol. For example, it confidently states, 'When the signal is given, the enslaved peoples of Europe will spring to action everywhere. The compact, fast-firing, easy-to-operate Sten gun will kill many Nazis behind the lines while the Allied armies fight on the newly opened fronts' (Anon 1943). Summing up the Sten, the article dramatically states:

> Faced with the problem of producing in quantities a gun simple enough to be operated by the untrained peasants who will become Europe's new guerrilla fighters, British ordnance experts threw out all previous notions of armament making and came up with this gun that made orthodox military thinkers gasp. But even the skeptics gave in when they saw the ugly duckling in action. Capable of firing 500 to 550 rounds a minute, this sturdy, six-pound package of dynamite can be operated by a child. It doesn't even require oiling. (Anon 1943)

Of course, many of the Stens parachuted into Europe ended up in the hands of the Germans rather than the Resistance. In 'Invasion Gun', an 18 September 1943 article in *Collier's* magazine, Harry Henderson and Sam Shaw describe the first reactions of a German patrol to a Sten gun captured in Norway in 1942:

> Returning to their barracks, the Nazi patrol assembled the gun. It consisted of four simple pieces: an all-metal stock, a nine-inch barrel, a piece of sheet-metal tubing containing the spring-backed breech and ejector, and a magazine holding thirty-two 9-mm. bullets. Not even the

detailed instructions accompanying the gun were needed to assemble it. On firing it, the Nazis discovered the gun could shoot faster than their own Schmeisser machine gun – 550 rounds per minute, and that it was amazingly accurate for so short a rifle. Within twenty-four hours, Reichskommissar Josef Terboven, head of the Nazi forces of occupation in Norway, had broadcast a decree of death for anyone found with a Sten gun. This was the the first time the world learned that the British had begun the task of arming the people of Europe so that they could effectively revolt when the Allied Armies landed in their territory.

Since then, the Berlin radio has yammered frequently that the British have been dropping the Sten 'in mass quantities.' This is, of course, 'a hideous crime' to the Nazis, who hate to think of meeting armed civilians. According to the Nazis, the guns have been dropped by the thousands in France, Yugoslavia, Greece, and Norway. (Henderson & Shaw 1943: 62)

As a result of Sten drops that had gone astray, Otto Skorzeny, the best-known German special-forces officer of World War II, had a chance to evaluate the Sten and was very impressed with it, especially the suppressed version. In *Skorzeny's Secret Missions*, he comments on the suppressed Sten: 'We gathered that the British also possessed a 'silencer' for these pistols but that it was still a top-secret weapon. This fact, of course, served only to incite me the more keenly to lay my hands on this device' (Skorzeny 1950: 25). Skorzeny hoped to acquire one among the captured Stens but could not; hence, he used a double agent to obtain a suppressed Sten in June 1943, presumably one of the SOE Mk II (S) versions. He comments upon the suppressed Sten: 'What splendid possibilities the use of these silencers offered, I thought enthusiastically. What losses they might save and what dangers they might avert! How wonderful, in case of an unexpected meeting with an enemy detachment, to be able to fire without the reports attracting the attention of other enemy groups!' (Skorzeny 1950: 26).

Skorzeny submitted the suppressed Sten to the German Armaments Research Office, but they were not interested. Skorzeny, with his flair for the dramatic, however, staged a demonstration for high-ranking officers:

While we were strolling in the park – night had already fallen – a soldier who walked several paces behind us fired off a whole clip and my lofty companions were astounded when I pointed to the empty cases that strewed the ground. Nevertheless, they raised several objections. The force of the recoil seemed to them to be unsatisfactory and they asserted that the silencer impaired accuracy in firing. (Skorzeny 1950: 26)

Winston Churchill takes aim with a Mk II during a visit to the Royal Artillery experimental station at Shoeburyness, Essex, 13 June 1941. (IWM H 10688)

The Sten in civilian hands

The Sten also saw some civilian sales after World War II. In Great Britain, at some point some Stens were converted to semi-automatic and sold for civilian sporting purposes. The author remembers attending the European International Practical Shooting Confederation Championships at Warminster, Wiltshire, right after the 1982 Falklands War and in the pavilion erected for vendors seeing dozens of converted semi-automatic Stens for sale. In the USA, the Sten has been sold in various configurations to conform to US firearms laws. Prior to 1986, when US laws regarding automatic weapons were revised to limit the number of transferable 'machine guns' in circulation, various Class III manufacturers fabricated selective-fire versions of the Sten using surplus parts and newly manufactured receivers (tubes). Some were sold to law-enforcement agencies and some were sold to US collectors who registered the weapons under the regulations of the National Firearms Act. After 1986, those Stens legally owned prior to that point could still be transferred to a collector who filed the proper paper work and paid the $200 tax. However, two other versions of the Sten can still be sold to collectors. A Sten that has been fabricated with a new receiver and that can only function as a semi-automatic may still be sold with the original Sten barrel if registered as a 'Short Barreled Rifle' under the National Firearms Act. Finally, a semi-automatic Sten with a 16in barrel may be sold as a carbine or if sold without a stock may keep the short barrel and be sold as a pistol. These versions would not fall under the National Firearms Act. The above is a simplified explanation of Stens sold on the US collector and shooter market. Anyone considering the purchase of a 'carbine' or 'pistol' version of the Sten would be wise to carefully consult local and federal laws.

Skorzeny also pointed out that the Sten was easier to manufacture and stood up to abuse better than German submachine guns, and that it required fewer raw materials. That he preferred the Sten to the elegant MP 38 or MP 40 was viewed as heresy. Those German soldiers who encountered the Sten in combat conditions were less impressed, as Leutnant Martin Poppel, a Fallschirmjäger who fought against British airborne troops in Sicily in 1943, attests when recalling the state of captured British troops:

> Certainly not eager to fight and their equipment looks fairly pathetic. The uniform resembles our motor vehicle combinations, though the camouflaging of the steel helmet looks useful, and their footwear is generally old and worn out. The guns look pathetic, reminding us of Russian weapons. Simply knocked together, the muzzle sight consisting of just an emergency sighting bar ... Their whole weaponry, ammunition and machines, comes mainly from America. (Poppel 2000: 123)

Like Poppel, many Germans may have felt that the crude Sten did not match the quality of the MP 38/40, but the necessities of war combined with the substantial number of Stens captured after stray airdrops caused the Sten to see considerable use by German rear-area security units and Nazi collaborators across Europe. In German service, the Mk I was designated the MP 748 (e), where 'e' stood for 'English'; the Mk II was termed the MP 749 (e), the Mk III the MP 750 (e), and the Mk V the MP 751 (e).

The Germans even built their own copies; almost 10,000 Sten Mk II copies were manufactured at Mauser Werke in Oberndorf-am-Neckar during late 1944 and early 1945. Designated the Potsdam *Gerät* (device), only two examples are known today, with the fate of the remainder a mystery.

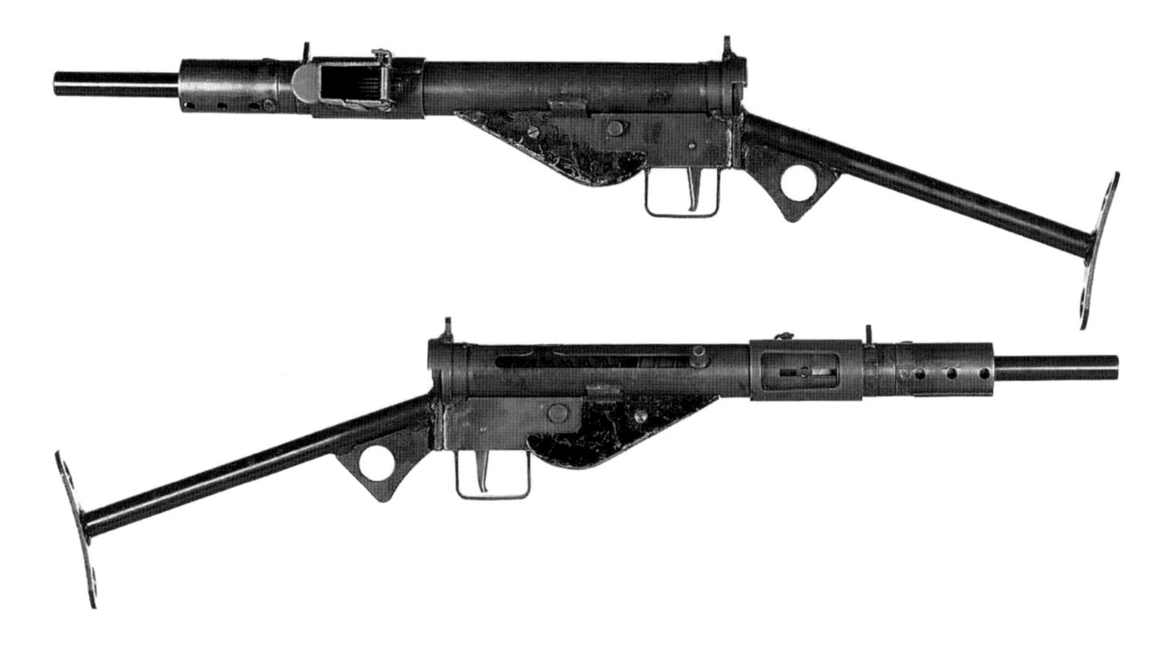

Another German version of the Sten, the MP 3008 'People's Machine Pistol', was a further simplified version; it used a bottom-feed MP 38/40 magazine and eliminated the barrel shroud. Although initial production of 50,000 MP 3008s was planned, it is estimated that a maximum of 10,000 were built. It most likely saw some combat with the Volkssturm, the last-ditch national militia thrown into combat by the Nazis in the closing months of the war in Europe.

The Potsdam *Gerät*, a German copy of the Sten, was produced as a 'last ditch' weapon late in World War II. (Copyright Collector Grade Publications, Inc.)

THE USA EVALUATES THE STEN

Shortly after the United States entered World War II, US Ordnance personnel evaluated the Mk II Sten:

> Guns in the STEN series had been tested at Aberdeen Proving Ground and had been criticized because of their highly unorthodox appearance. The STEN demonstrated, however, that an efficient submachine gun could be made at small unit cost and by rapid production-line methods. Officers of the Small Arms Development Branch realized that in modern warfare there are other criteria than mere appearance. They knew that huge numbers of weapons of this type would be required and directed all efforts toward the production of a gun which could be manufactured as easily, as swiftly, and as economically as the STEN. (Nelson 1977: 490)

Though the USA did not adopt the Sten, other than some suppressed versions obtained for use by OSS (see page 49), it seems obvious that the development of the M3 submachine gun, known among GIs as the 'Grease Gun' for its resemblance to the device used to apply grease to automobiles, was influenced by the Sten. The M3 was adopted by the US Army on

This early Enfield-production Mk II with 'T'-stock was sent to the USA for evaluation. (Copyright Collector Grade Publications, Inc.)

12 December 1942. It had been developed from an October 1942 study by the Ordnance Department on development of a 'Sten-type' submachine gun. Based on requirements submitted by the Army, a sheet-metal weapon in .45 ACP designed for fast, inexpensive production requiring minimal machining was developed. The M3 was designed to fire in either semi- or full-automatic mode and used a heavy bolt to keep its cyclic rate under 500rpm.

M3 submachine guns were manufactured at the General Motors Guide Lamp Division, with a total of 606,694 being produced between 1943 and 1945. Based on problems encountered in the field with the M3, an improved version, the M3A1, was introduced in December 1944. Before the end of the war, 15,469 M3A1s were produced. Though intended to replace the Thompson submachine gun, the latter continued in use until the end of World War II.

The M3 remained in service with US troops until the early 1990s. Delta Force, the US counterterrorist force based on the British Special Air Service, upon its foundation late in 1977 chose the M3 as its first

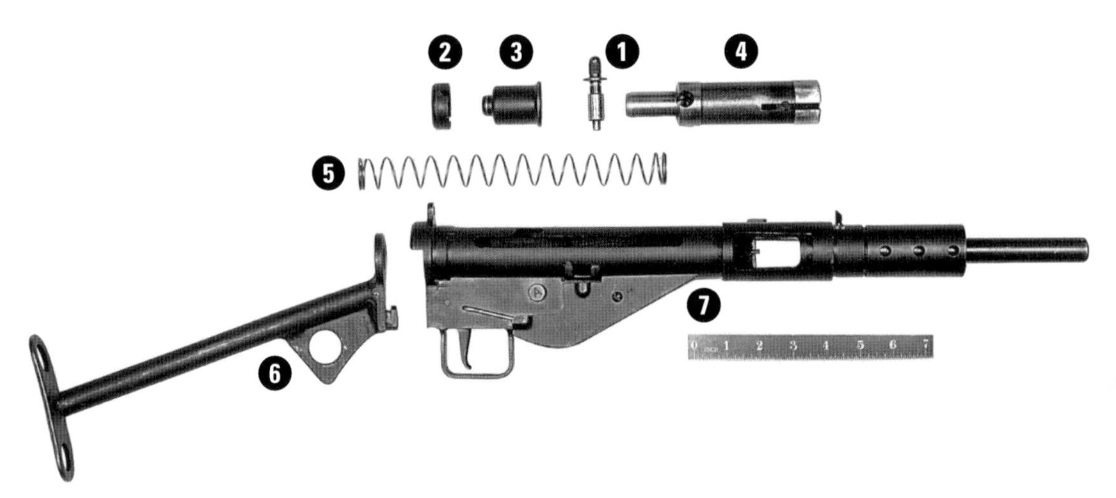

The Enfield Sten sent to the USA for evaluation is shown here disassembled: **(1)** cocking handle; **(2)** return-spring cap; **(3)** return-spring housing; **(4)** breech block; **(5)** return spring; **(6)** stock; **(7)** receiver and barrel. (Copyright Collector Grade Publications, Inc.)

submachine gun and, as did many other special-operations personnel, liked its slow rate of fire, which made it very controllable to fire and easy to keep on target during full-automatic fire.

For the OSS, which would be operating in areas where German 9mm ammunition would be more readily acquired than .45 ACP, the Guide Lamp Division of General Motors produced 9mm conversion kits for the M3. These kits were designed to use Sten magazines. The figure normally given for the number of these conversion kits produced is 200.

Brittany, France, 28 August 1944: a left-handed US soldier armed with an M3 'grease gun' covers a captured German soldier. When held left-handed, the location of the ejection port on the M3 meant it would be less likely to throw hot brass in the face than the Sten would. (NARA)

Another country that produced a version of the Sten was Nationalist China. This copy of the Mk II Sten was designated the M38 and turned up during the Korean War in substantial numbers in the hands of Chinese and North Korean troops. Apparently, the Communists captured machinery to produce the M38 when they drove the Nationalists from China, while after 1950 the Nationalists produced the M38 on Taiwan. Later, the Chinese Communists converted a substantial number of M38s to fire the 7.62×25mm Tokarev cartridge, the round used in the Soviet-designed World War II-era PPSh-41 and PPS-43 submachine guns.

Among other foreign manufacturers of the Sten were Argentina, which produced the Modelo C.4., and France, which produced the R5. Indonesia seems to have produced a crude 'jungle workshop' Sten using salvaged and reworked parts. Some of these turned up in Malaya. Both India and Pakistan used vast numbers of Stens in conflicts after 1945. On 31 October 1984, two Sikh soldiers, one armed with a Sten, assassinated Indira Gandhi, the prime minister of India. The assassination was carried out in retaliation for Operation *Blue Star*, an attack by government forces, including tanks, on Sikh separatists in Amritsar earlier that year.

REPLACING THE STEN

During the immediate postwar years there were many Stens remaining in armouries, and with the downsizing of the British armed forces there was little impetus to adopt a new submachine gun. During World War II, though, the Ordnance Board had continued to look at other submachine-gun designs. On 25 September 1942, George William Patchett submitted a design to the Ordnance Board that retained many features of the Lanchester, though it originally lacked a butt and sights and was intended for firing from the hip. Also different from the Lanchester was the trigger group; it incorporated a selector switch that could be set on single, auto or Safe. When on Safe, the breech block was locked in the forward position. In designing the new submachine gun, Patchett was attempting to create a weapon that was lighter and handier, more reliable and safer than other submachine-gun designs available at the time.

After a butt and sights were added, it was introduced into British service in 1944 as the Sterling submachine gun, incorporating improvements over the Sten including a more comfortable stock, pistol grip and full-length ventilated handguard. The Sterling was also more reliable than the Sten, at least partially due to its much-improved 34-round double-column curved magazine. Very few Sterlings actually saw combat during World War II, though, and those that did were often labelled the 'Patchett' after the gun's designer.

However, after a series of trials between 1947 and 1951, the Sterling was developed further, adopted, and entered service to replace the Sten in 1953 as the L2A1 Submachine Gun. It would remain in service for more than 40 years until 1994. A suppressed version – the L34A1 – entered service in 1966 and was widely used by British special-operations units until replaced by the MP5SD. At the time of writing, some L34A1s remain in UK reserve stocks.

The Sterling was eventually adopted by more than 40 countries, many of them in the Commonwealth or with ties to the United Kingdom. Among the larger foreign purchasers of Sterlings were: Ceylon, now Sri Lanka (2,260), Ghana (5,990), India (32,536), Iraq (13,311), Kenya (2,297), Kuwait (4,437), Libya (3,095), Malaysia (18,463), New Zealand (2,006), Nigeria (5,844), Portugal (2,032) and Tunisia (4,660). At least some countries continue to use the Sterling or have it in reserve. Though superseded in many armies by the HK MP5 or within the Russian sphere of influence by the AKSU-74, the Sterling has continued in use with many military units into the 21st century. A substantial number of special-warfare units adopted the L34A1 and used it for many years, though many have since replaced it with the HK MP5SD.

A left-side view of a Mk IV Sterling with stock extended and single magazine fitted. (C&S)

CONCLUSION

The Sten gun doesn't rank among the safest or most reliable submachine guns. Nor is it a beautiful example of gunmaking like the Thompson. In most ways the Sten was not particularly user-friendly, though some would argue that point in the case of the Mk V. Simply, the Sten was far from optimal.

However, what the Sten *was* was the right weapon at the right time. Britain was in dire circumstances when the Sten was designed. The possibility of German invasion loomed and raw materials and industrial capacity were scarce; so was cash. Supplies of the Thompson submachine gun could not meet demand, and its cost was prohibitive. Even the Thompson's .45 ACP ammunition was more expensive and used more metal than the 9mm Parabellum cartridge. Plus, the 9mm was the standard pistol and submachine-gun cartridge of the German Army, and thus captured supplies could be readily used by British stay-behind parties or the Home Guard should invasion come. British airborne troops would be operating behind German lines as well and could add captured ammunition to their basic load.

For the purposes of the Home Guard, the Sten was certainly a better weapon than pitchforks or sporting shotguns. In many ways, the mass-produced submachine gun is the perfect 'people's weapon' for fighting in urban areas or ambushing the enemy at close range. Simo Häyhä, the Finnish master sniper of the Winter War, was a hunter and farmer in peacetime, not a soldier by profession; he actually achieved more of his staggering 500 kills (in 100 days' fighting) with his Suomi submachine gun than with his M1928 Mosin-Nagant rifle (Jowett & Snodgrass 2006: 44–45). And, certainly, the Soviets killed a lot of Germans with their PPSh-41 and PPS-43 submachine guns, the latter designed for cheap and fast production like the Sten. Whether it was the PPS-43, the Sten, or the M3 'Grease Gun', killing the enemy was considered a good thing, killing them cheaply even better!

One of the most common criticisms of the Sten, especially the models before the Mk V, was its propensity for negligent or accidental discharges. I have read numerous accounts of the Sten wounding or killing British troops during the war. As a person who has carried loaded pistols, rifles, shotguns and submachine guns for most of his adult life, I can say that most of those incidents could have been avoided. The problem was, and still is, that soldiers and law-enforcement officers get complacent. They get sloppy about the principle of always treating each weapon as loaded and dangerous. The Sten's tendency to go off if the cocking handle jarred out of the safety slot or the stock was given a hard bump when the bolt was forward was well known. Troops usually made the conscious choice to keep the Sten with a magazine in place, based on the assumption that they might need it quickly. It might, then, be argued that more troops were saved by having their Sten ready when an enemy was suddenly encountered than were injured by accident. The Sten was more dangerous to its users than most infantry weapons, but all weapons are dangerous.

Anecdotally, a criticism of the Sten was that the firer's left little finger could stray into the ejection port and be severed. Sten authority Peter Laidler actually carried out tests in conjunction with physicians from the Physical Anatomy Deparment of a medical school. He found that even when the bolt came forward from full cock it would not sever the finger. He also relates his own experience during the tests of having the bolt drop on his finger from full cock. Although severing the finger appears to have been unlikely, bruising or cuts certainly could occur. Like US troops who learned how to avoid 'Garand Thumb', users of the Sten would learn to take care over their placement of the left hand when firing.

My personal view of the Sten is mixed. As has already been stated, its shortcomings were overshadowed by Britain's need for an inexpensive mass-produced weapon, fast. No invading German wanted to be shot by a Sten or anything else. Since support troops are usually busy performing other tasks, a compact weapon such as the Sten allowed them to be armed with a weapon that may be carried and stowed easily – the mission of today's PDW (Personal Defence Weapon). For soldiers parachuting into combat, the Sten offered a compromise that addressed the question faced by airborne troops since their inception: is it better to have a weapon with which it is easy to jump and which offers less chance of injury during landing, or one that is more powerful? And, for those with a raiding or *coup de main* mission, the Sten's firepower was a great advantage.

I have mostly used the Mk II Sten, which I found adequate but not excellent. Among World War II submachine guns I would rate the Suomi and Owen superior, but I would rather carry the lighter Sten! I have only had a couple of chances to fire the Mk V Sten, but when I did my opinion of the Sten was raised notably. I use the elegant HK MP5 quite a bit and find it an excellent weapon, but had I been in the Home Guard in 1942 I would have been quite happy to receive my Sten.

During Britain's darkest hour, the Sten was there should it be necessary to fight on the beaches, on the landing grounds, in the fields, in the streets, and in the hills. It would have armed the British Resistance, and it did arm many other Resistance movements. Love it or hate it, the Sten has earned its place as one of the best-known weapons of World War II.

FURTHER READING

Anonymous (no date). *The Sten Machine Carbine*. Aldershot: Gale & Polden Ltd, no date (reprint by The Naval and Military Press Ltd of a copy in the Royal Armouries Museum collection).

Anonymous (1942a). *Small Arms Training, Volume I, Pamphlet No. 22: Sten Machine Carbine*. August 1942.

Anonymous (1942b). *Sten Machine Carbine, 9mm. Mk. II and Mk. III*. 4th edition. Bradford-on-Avon: The Bravon Ledger Co., September 1942.

Anonymous (1943). 'Sten Gun to be Forerunner of Invasion', *Popular Science*, September 1943, pp. 54–55.

Anonymous (1962). 'Malaysia: Fighting the Federation', *Time* magazine, 21 December 1962.

Bailey, Roderick (2008a). *The Wildest Province: SOE in the Land of the Eagle*. London: Jonathan Cape.

Bailey, Roderick (ed.) (2008b). *Forgotten Voices of the Secret War: An Inside History of Special Operations during the Second World War*. London: Ebury.

Baldwin, William W. (1957). *Mau-Mau Manhunt*. New York, NY: E.P. Dutton & Co.

Barber, Neil (2009). *The Pegasus and Orne Bridges: Their Capture, Defence and Relief on D-Day*. Barnsley: Pen & Sword.

Bijl, Nick van der (2010). *The Cyprus Emergency: The Divided Island 1955–1974*. Barnsley: Pen & Sword.

Bouchery, Jean (2001). *The British Soldier from D-Day to VE-Day, Volume 2: Organisation, Armament, Tanks and Vehicles*. Paris: Histoire & Collections.

Brayley, Martin J. (2001). Men-at-Arms 354: *The British Army 1939–45 (1): North-West Europe*. Oxford: Osprey.

Brayley, Martin J. (2002a). Men-at-Arms 368: *The British Army 1939–45 (2): Middle East & Mediterranean*. Oxford: Osprey.

Brayley, Martin J. (2002b). Men-at-Arms 375: *The British Army 1939–45 (3): The Far East*. Oxford: Osprey.

Brown, Robert K. (1959). 'They "Rolled their Own" in Cuba', *Guns* magazine. October 1959, 17.

Bull, Stephen (2007). Elite 151: *World War II Jungle Warfare Tactics*. Oxford: Osprey.

Cavenagh, Sandy (1965). *Airborne to Suez*. London: William Kimber.

Chappell, Mike (2000). Men-at-Arms 108: *British Infantry Equipments (2): 1908–2000* (revised edition). Oxford: Osprey.

Chartrand, René (2001). Men-at-Arms 359: *Canadian Forces in World War II*. Oxford: Osprey.

Clark, Lloyd (2009). *Arnhem: Jumping the Rhine 1944 and 1945 – The Greatest Airborne Battle in History*. London: Headline Review.

Clough, Marshall S. (1997). *Mau Mau Memoirs: History, Memory, and Politics*. Boulder, CO: Lynne Rienner Publishers.

Coogan, Tim Pat (1993). *The IRA: A History*. Niwot, CO: Roberts Publishing Company Ltd.

Defelice, Jim (2008). *Rangers at Dieppe: The First Combat Action of U.S. Army Rangers in World War II*. New York, NY: Berkley Publishing.

Doyle, Peter (2005). Shire Library 447: *The Victoria Cross*. Princes Risborough: Shire.

Foot, M.R.D. (1999). *SOE: The Special Operations Executive 1940–1946*. London: Pimlico.

Forty, Lt Col George (ed.) (2009). *Jake Wardrop's Diary: A Tank Regiment Sergeant's Story*. Stroud: Amberley.

Gordon, David B. (2004). *Weapons of the WWII Tommy*. Missoula, MT: Pictorial Histories Publishing Co.

Gorton, Bruce (2011). 'The Kiwi Sten', International *Arms & Militaria Collector*, Annual No. 29, pp. 128–29.

Green, David (2003). *Captured at the Imjin River: The Korean War Memoirs of a Gloster 1950–1953*. Barnsley: Pen & Sword.

Harclerode, Peter (1992). *Para! Fifty Years of the Parachute Regiment*. London: Arms & Armour Press.

Henderson, Harry & Sam Shaw (1943). 'Invasion Gun', *Collier's Magazine*, 18 September 1943, pp. 62–65.

Hobart, F.W.A. (1973). *Pictorial History of the Sub-Machine Gun*. New York, NY: Charles Scribner's Sons.

Huff, Roland (1986). *The Sten Machine Gun: Operational Manual*. El Dorado, AR: Desert Publications.

Johnston, Mark (2007). Elite 153: *The Australian Army in World War II*. Oxford: Osprey.

Jowett, Philip & Brent Snodgrass (2006). Elite 141: *Finland at War 1939–45*. Oxford: Osprey.

Kent, Ron (1979). *First In: A history of the 21st Independent Parachute Company, the original pathfinders of the British Airborne Forces, 1942–1946*. London: B.T. Batsford Ltd.

Laidler, Peter (1995). *The Guns of Dagenham: Lanchester/Patchett/ Sterling*. Cobourg: Collector Grade Publications.

Laidler, Peter (2000). *The Sten Machine Carbine*. Cobourg: Collector Grade Publications.

Longmate, Norman (1974). *The Real Dad's Army: The Story of the Home Guard*. London: Arrow Books.

Middlebrook, Martin (1995). *Arnhem 1944: The Airborne Battle*. London: Penguin Viking.

Milstein, Uri (1997). *History of the War of Independence, Vol. 2: The First Month*. Lanham, MD: University Press of America.

Morgan, Mike (2004). *D-Day Hero: CSM Stanley Hollis VC*. Stroud: Sutton Publishing.

Myatt, Maj Frederick (1981). *An Illustrated Guide to Rifles and Sub-Machine Guns*. London: Salamander.

Nelson, Thomas B. (1977). *The World's Submachine Guns (Machine Pistols)*. Alexandra, VA: TBN Enterprises.

Nichol, John & Tony Rennell (2011). *Arnhem: The Battle for Survival*. London: Penguin Viking.

O'Riain, Bernard (2005). *Running to Stand Still: The Compassionate Heart of a Violent Man – a Unique Account of Abuse*. Johannesburg: Jacana Media (Pty) Ltd.

Plaster, John L. (2000). *SOG: A Photo History of the Secret Wars*. Boulder, CO: Paladin Press.

Poppel, Martin (2000). *Heaven and Hell: The War Diary of a German Paratrooper*. Staplehurst: Spellmount.

Powell, Geoffrey (1998). *Men at Arnhem*. Barnsley: Leo Cooper.

Salmon, Andrew (2009). *To the Last Round: The Epic British Stand on the Imjin River, Korea 1951*. London: Aurum.

Sapp, Darren (no date). 'Aaron Bank and the Early Days of the U.S. Army Special Forces'. Master's thesis available at <https://sites.google.com/site/aaronbankspecforces/>

Saunders, Hilary St George (1952). *The Red Beret: The Story of the Parachute Regiment at War, 1940–45*. London: Michael Joseph.

Skorzeny, Otto (1950). *Skorzeny's Secret Missions*. New York, NY: E.P. Dutton & Co.

Stacey, Col C.P. (1948). *The Canadian Army 1939–1945: An Official Historical Summary*. Ottawa: Edmond Cloutier.

Stacey, Col C.P. (1960). *Official History of the Canadian Army in the Second World War, Volume III: The Victory Campaign. The Operations in North-West Europe 1944–45*. Ottawa: Queen's Printer.

Sumner, Ian & François Vauvillier (1998a). Men-at-Arms 315: *The French Army 1939–45 (1)*. Oxford: Osprey.

Sumner, Ian & François Vauvillier (1998b). Men-at-Arms 318: *The French Army 1939–45 (2)*. Oxford: Osprey.

Thompson, Julian (2010). *Forgotten Voices of Burma: The Second World War's Forgotten Conflict*. London: Ebury.

Tout, Ken (2000). *The Bloody Battle for Tilly: Normandy 1944*. Stroud: Sutton Publishing.

Tout, Ken (2003). *In the Shadow of Arnhem: The Battle for the Lower Maas, September–November 1944*. Stroud: Sutton Publishing.

Turner, Barry (2006). *Suez 1956: The Inside Story of the First Oil War*. London: Hodder.

Warrack, Graeme (1968). *Travel By Dark After Arnhem*. London: Harvill Press.

Warwicker, John (2008). *Churchill's Underground Army: A History of the Auxiliary Units in World War II*. London: Frontline Books.

Williams, Neville (2009). *A Conscript in Korea*. Barnsley: Pen & Sword.

Wilson, David (1998). *Always First: The RAAF Airfield Construction Squadrons, 1942–1974*. Canberra: Air Power Studies Centre.

Wood, Lt Col H.F. (1966). *Strange Battleground: The Operations in Korea and their Effects on the Defence Policy of Canada*. Ottawa: Roger Duhamel.

INDEX

Page numbers in **bold** refer to illustrations